She Rise.

A Book of Strength

Turning Wounds into Wisdom and Endurance into a Way of Life

By: Dr. S.C.C. Hooks

Copyright © 2025 by Dr. Sherrise C. Cohen-Hooks

All rights reserved. No part of this publication may be reproduced, stored in a retrieval system, or transmitted in any form or by any means—electronic, mechanical, photocopying, recording, or otherwise—without prior written permission from the author, except in the case of brief quotations used in reviews, articles, or educational purposes as permitted by law.

This work has been prayerfully and prophetically curated by Dr. Sherrise C. Cohen-Hooks with a commitment to inspire healing, ignite truth, and equip rising vessels with language, strategy, and victory. All images, illustrations, references, and spiritual reflections have been carefully selected to support the message and journey of this work. Mentions of cultural figures such as Lalah Hathaway, Maya Angelou, *The Truman Show*, Mowgli, and Walt Disney are for inspirational and illustrative purposes only and do not imply any association, endorsement, or partnership.

Unless otherwise noted, all scripture quotations are taken from the King James Version (KJV) of the Bible, which is in the public domain.

"She Rise" is a protected phrase and movement authored by Dr. Sherrise C. Cohen-Hooks. All expressions related to the "She Rise" journey—including titles, declarations, visual concepts, and thematic language—are proprietary and may not be duplicated, adapted, or distributed without written consent from the author.

Published by Elevated Connection, LLC

United States of America

ISBN: 979-8-9999047-0-6

Printed in the United States of America

First Edition – 20

Dedication

To my mother,
Thank you for naming me with a name that would forever remind me of who I am, my purpose, and my destiny. I'm sure you didn't know then just how prophetic it would be—or that you wouldn't still be here to witness the growth it would represent. Though I have grieved you deeply through the years, my heart is now open and willing to be released so you can see the greatness you brought into the earth. I honor and celebrate you, Virginia E. Cohen.

To my father,
Though our time together was limited, I honor the part of me that comes from you. Your DNA gifted me with strength, determination, and a fighter's heart. In spite of all things, you were part of the reason I'm here—and for that, I am grateful.

To my husband,
Thank you for your support and encouragement. You always believed I would do great things. You always believed I could help anyone. So here's my try. Your quiet strength has been a covering to my calling.

To my boys,
I love you beyond words. You are the reason I fight, the heartbeat of my mission, and the proof that purpose bears fruit. You mean the world to me, and I am constantly inspired by your lives. You are legacy in motion. I see you. I carry you. I rise for you.

With all my heart,

—She Rise

Acknowledgments

To my sons, my niece-daughters, my daughters by sons, god-children, Gaga's kiddos, and my grandchildren—you are the reason I keep going. Whether born to me, chosen by me, or bound through covenant, each of you holds a sacred place in my heart. You are legacy, laughter, and love in living form. Your very existence reminds me why I rise, why I fight, and why I build.
To my church,

Thank you for being my chalkboard. You have allowed me to walk through the blueprint of what God has called me to build—with grace, with patience, and with love. You have been the soil where so much revelation has been planted, watered and made to grow.

To My Pastor and Fellow Leaders,

Thank you for the prayers, wisdom, encouragement, and spiritual insight that you have poured into my life across the years. Whether through a preached word, a moment of counsel, or simply standing in obedience to your own call, you helped shape my hunger for truth and my commitment to the Kingdom. I am grateful for your leadership, your labor, and your willingness to serve. May your continued obedience cause others to rise, just as your example helped me do the same.

To my extended family—whether blood, created, or inherited (in-laws),

Thank you for loving me, covering me, and walking with me through seasons of silence, victory, and vision. Some of you share my name, some joined my name, and some simply share my journey—but each of you has shared my becoming. That is family at its deepest level. I love you!!!

And finally, to the LoveJoys—my created family, the builders of legacy, and the keepers of my greatest traditions. You are living proof that family is not only inherited but also cultivated, nurtured, and chosen. Through you, I see continuity, strength, and joy carried forward. You are my reminder that what God establishes in love will stand for generations.

To every soul who poured into me down through the years, encouraged me, interceded for me, or simply stood near—whether your name is written here or not, your love and presence helped birth this moment.

To my Freunde, confidant, and intercessor who carried me in prayer, pushed me toward purpose, pulled me out of hiding, and spoke into the release of my gifts—

through your love, friendship, and intercession, I have learned to live more openly, more boldly, and more fully in what God has called me to do. And from that place, I push forward purpose, strength, and hope for those who will come after me.

To my assistant—You already know my gratitude. Thank you for standing with me, for the unseen sacrifices, and for helping me carry the weight of vision.

To my entire team—I honor you not for the size of the task, but for the spirit of preparation, for this is only the beginning. Greater work, greater stretching, and greater glory are ahead. Thank you for preparing for all that God will do.

For every book I began and never finished, every manuscript I completed but never published, and every word I stored in the hidden archives of my mind or computer—thank You, Lord, for pressing me through to birth this one. This is the book we were waiting for. And may its rising be the unfolding of all the books still to come.

Most of all, God—You are my first thought and my final word. It is because of You, and in You, that I live, move, breathe, and have my being. Thank You for it all. I make no complaint; I trust Your authorship of my life, highs, lows, loss and gain; I trust Your process and Your timing. I love You with all of me. Here is my worship.

Table of Contents (Your Rise Map)

To the One Who's Rising in Real Time – 1

Authors Note – 3

Before You Begin: A Gentle Pause – 6

What's behind a Name?! Everything –10

Beginning of the Rise

She Rise: Wilderness – Part I: The Process was the Wilderness - 15

She Rise in Silence – 22

She Rise While Weeping –28

She Rise with Strategy – 37

She Rise: From Storm to Endurance, Formed Like a Snowflake – 49

Because She Rise Healed – 55

She Rise in Morph: Honoring the Hidden Transformations – 66

Because She Rise, She Defeated the Odds – 80

She Rise: The Anatomy of My Becoming – 86

She Rise with Tools – 96

Borndage: Breaking Birth Bound Chains – 104

Core of the Rise

Depth of the Rise – 116

Hard Choices and Holy Returns: She Rise: Truth – 124

She Rise with Voice – 131

She Rise Word of Fire: Your Emotions Are Not Your Altar – 137

The Rise of Obedience: Seeing Without Sight – 147

What Rising Looks Like on Empty – 157

She Rise Through the Wilderness–Part II – 167

From Wilderness to Wind: The Rise Doesn't End, It Deepen – 180

Final Lift

She Rise Lessons Learned – 184

She Rise with Strength – 197

She Rise in Consciousness – 210

She Rise: Find the Reason – 221

She Rise in Revolution – 232

Beyond the Rise
The Journey Continues

To the One Who's Rising Anyway – 243

Personal Declaration: I Rise/ I Rise Whole– 246

Guardrails for the Journey – 249

Closing Letter: For My Rise to Yours

Final Whisper for a Hungry Heart –

References for Deeper Study & Confirmation

About the Author

To the One Who's Rising in Real Time

If this book found its way into your hands, I believe it was guided by something greater than coincidence.

You're holding more than pages—you're holding evidence. Evidence that rising is still possible. That strength can still be born from silence. That tears do not cancel the assignment. That pain is not the end of your story—it's the beginning of your becoming.

I wrote this not to impress you, but to meet you. Wherever you are—in a storm, in a stretch of silence, in a space between your breaking and your building—I want you to know: you are not alone, and you are not forgotten.

Every word in this book is soaked in reality and revival. These pages carry the rhythm of my own rise—through betrayal, abandonment, fire, grief, and sacred growth. I didn't write from theory. I wrote from testimony. From Harlem to healing, from weeping to walking with wisdom—I am still rising. And so are you.

You don't have to explain your pain to everyone.

You don't have to perform your progress.

You don't have to shrink to survive.

You just have to keep getting up.

Let this be your portable prophecy. Let this be your pocket reminder that your rising is not random—it's rebuilding something eternal.

And when the world asks, "How you made it?",

Let your fruit speak.

Let your fire guide.

Let your life prove it.

With oil in my hands, and truth in my bones, She Rise, and so will you.

—Dr. Sherrise C. Cohen-Hooks

Author's Note: Let Me Be Clear

If you've ever heard me preach, teach, or even sit in conversation—you already know one thing about me.

I repeat myself.

And I don't apologize for it.

Not because I don't have anything new to say, but because the truth doesn't expire.

I have been saying the same things for years—yet with deeper revelation.

And I will keep saying them until we become what we've heard, because consistency is the key to impartation.

This is how I move.

This is how I teach.

This is how I rise.

But hear me clearly: as you turn these pages, you will notice that I move between I and She. This is not confusion—it is intention. When I say I, it is my testimony, my lived story, my voice rising in its own oil. When I say She, it is not only me—it is the witness within me, it is the strength within you, it is every soul who has ever been called to rise.

I is confession.

She is becoming.

I speak of what has already been walked.

She calls forth what is still unfolding.

This rhythm matters, because impartation is not a one-time moment—it is consistency that presses truth into the spirit until it sticks. What may look like repetition is really revelation evolving. I do not just recycle words—I water seeds. She does not just hear words—she becomes the garden.

Not because I ran out of words, but because God hasn't run out of grace.

And because sometimes you need to hear it again in a new season—so the deeper revelation hidden inside of it can finally be caught.

I write like I speak.

I speak like I live—with conviction, with care, and with a calling to help you rise.

She listens like she is becoming—with hunger, with hope, with the oil of endurance.

So if you find something said again, sit with it.

It might be what brings the breakthrough this time.

Let's go deeper—together.

Same truth. New oil.

One rise at a time.

—Dr. Sherrise C. Cohen-Hooks ~ She Rise

Before You Begin: A Gentle Pause

This isn't just a book. It's a place.

A resting place. A stretching place.

A place where oil and reality meet.

Before you move forward, take a breath.

Still yourself.

Invite the Lord in.

This isn't about reading to finish.

It's about reading to feel.

Reading to receive.

Reading to return.

I wrote from my own rise—not to impress you,

but to remind you that you're not alone in yours.

So, before you turn the page, ask yourself:

Am I willing to let God speak here—right where I am?

You may weep.

You may wrestle.

You may breathe a little deeper than you have in months. That's okay.

This isn't about performance.

It's about presence.

And healing doesn't ask you to be ready.

It just asks you to be willing.

Say this if you can:

"God, meet me in these words. Let what I'm holding rise into something holy. Speak to me gently, boldly, and personally. I receive."

Now, let's walk this together.

—She Rise

And now, as you turn these pages, may you enter not just my story but your own. This is not just a book — it is a journey of becoming, of breaking, of rising. Welcome to the Rise.

What's behind a Name?! Everything

My mother named me Sherrise. [shuh-REES]

And for years, I carried that name without knowing just how sacred it really was.

I always quoted Maya Angelou's "Still I Rise," feeling something in my soul every time those words came alive in my mouth. But it wasn't until 2024 that I looked at my own name and saw it for what it truly carried. Yes, there's an extra "R." But that "R" is more than just a letter—it's a sound. It's grit. It's pressure. It's fire in the belly before the rising.

She. Rrrr. Rise.

I didn't just see it—I heard it.

That middle "R" sounded like a growl... a roar... a rumble of power pushing up through pain.

It was a signal that something had survived. That something was emerging.

She roars, then she rises.

That's what I've done my whole life. And now, I don't just quote the rise—I embody it.

This isn't branding. This is birthing.

This is not a tagline. This is transformation.

So, when you see the words She Rise, know this isn't just a poetic phrase—it's my becoming.

And maybe, just maybe, it's yours too.
— She Rise

And let me pause here for a side note: names are never just names. We live in a world where people name-drop for advantage and status, but how many truly pay attention to what comes behind the name? When you look past the sound and into the soul, you see light, you discover strength, and you recognize essence. When someone calls you by name, your DNA speaks. Your heritage echoes. Your lineage rises to the surface. To be called by name is to be seen. That is why when God names you, it is not casual—it is compass and calling. His naming does not flatter; it directs. It does not decorate; it defines. Names are not given just to sound good; they carry weight, they reveal purpose, and they release destiny.

We don't just know a tree by its name—we know a tree by the fruit it bears. What is supposed to be seen on that tree is not confirmed by what it is called, but by what it produces. Jesus said, "Ye shall know them by their fruits... Even so every good tree bringeth forth good fruit; but a corrupt tree bringeth forth evil fruit" (Matthew 7:16–17 KJV). In the same way, your name alone is not your proof. It is the fruit you bear that validates the name you carry.

So, here's the reflection: What will your name produce? How will you be identified? Will your name echo as a title only, or will it testify of the life you lived, the fruit you bore, and the destiny you fulfilled? She Rise is not just about me—it's about what is being birthed in you, through you, and from you.

Don't just follow me on my journey. Let's find yours—with clarity.

She Rise: Wilderness –
Part I: The Wait Was the Wilderness

"Some rises don't look like rescue. They look like survival. They sound like silence. They feel like fire. Respect the wilderness."

There is a kind of becoming that only happens in barren places. The wilderness doesn't offer applause. It doesn't validate, it doesn't explain—it just exposes. It stretches. It waits for you to find out who you are when nothing grows. It asks you, "Can you still rise when nothing is blooming? Can you obey when nothing is opening? Can you stay faithful when your prayers are echoing off the walls of dry places?"

The wilderness is not punishment — it is the proving ground where survival turns into strength, and strength into destiny.

This is the wilderness—not as punishment, but as processing. A sacred suspension between the person you were, and the person God is forming. She doesn't rise quickly here. She rises slowly, deeply, honestly. She rises with her knees in the dirt and her hope tangled in holy delay. Because in this wilderness, rising isn't about arrival. It's about identity.

This isn't the last time you'll hear about the wilderness. In fact, it might just be the beginning. Because for some of us, wilderness isn't just a place we pass through, it's a language we learn to speak. It's a rhythm of becoming that keeps revealing new layers, even after we've left the dry places. So let this be your introduction. Later, you'll meet the other side of it.

The wait was never a denial. It was a divine invitation to break away from Egypt before stepping into Canaan. And even when the door didn't open, something else did—her understanding. She began to see that this wasn't rejection. This was refining. This wasn't God withholding—this was God with her in the silence, walking her out of the familiar so He could reintroduce her to the version of herself He always saw.

The wilderness became her womb. Every dry moment started to carry meaning. Every unanswered prayer started to become a mirror. Not because she had clarity—but because she had God's presence. And when the external broke down, the internal stood up. That's where she found her rise.

No one talks about how long the wilderness takes. It's not a weekend of inconvenience—it's a season of stripping. It's the divine timeline where God crushes your craving for control, and in the silence, teaches you to eat manna—not ambition. It's where you unlearn the voice of fear and start hearing the language of trust. It's where impatience starts dying, and intercession gets born. She had to realize—God doesn't operate in delay. He operates in design.

And design always takes time.

She was still, but she wasn't stuck. She was waiting, but she was becoming. Becoming what? Becoming who God intended.

Becoming more authentic.

Becoming more whole.

Becoming more disciplined.

Becoming more aligned.

Shaped by storms, formed by silence, filled with victory.

This wilderness was her seminary. Her school of the Spirit. Her sacred isolation. And the longer she stayed in it, the more her appetites changed. She no longer craved the quick win. She started craving His will. The girl who once begged for escape started asking for endurance. The woman who once questioned God's silence started seeing it as protection.

Yes, there were tears. Yes, there were days she didn't know what to pray. But even in that, she wasn't forsaken. Because God doesn't leave us in the wilderness to wander. He leads us there to wean us off of Egypt. To detox us from what fed us while also enslaving us. He brings us there to recalibrate our rhythm, our desires, our thoughts.

In the wilderness, she stopped performing. She stopped pretending. She learned how to walk slowly and trust deeply. She learned how to wait *well*—not just to wait long.

She thought she was waiting for a promise. But God was waiting on her posture. Because the promised land isn't just given to those who want it. It's given to those who've been formed to carry it.

She rose not by the speed of her deliverance, but by the stillness of her surrender. She rose through the wilderness not because it ended quickly, but because she learned to listen while it lasted.

To the one still wandering—know this: you're not lost, you're being led.

To the one still waiting—know this: the wait is not empty, it's holy.

To the one who thought delay meant denial—God is designing you for something weightier than quick results.

You are becoming even when nothing is blooming.

You are becoming even when silence is all you hear.

You are becoming because God still speaks in dry places.

And when the time comes to rise, you won't rise randomly—you'll rise with rhythm, with reverence, and with readiness.

Let the wilderness finish its work in you.
Then carry the weight of what only it could reveal.

She Rise, not because the wilderness ended, but because she discovered destiny in the dry place.

"Wilderness reveals who you are, but silence refines who you're willing to become."

You've come through the wilderness, but now you're being summoned into something quieter. Something deeper. Something that doesn't demand your response but invites your surrender. Silence is not absence. Silence is alignment. And in that stillness, a new level of rising begins—not in public, but in posture.

She Rise in Silence

"The silence wasn't punishment—it was preparation. I didn't lose my voice. I found my breath."

There are seasons in my life where God didn't say much—but He was doing everything. The silence didn't mean absence. It meant intention. In fact, silence has become one of His most sacred tools in my life. He has used it to protect me, to prepare me, and most of all, to preserve what He's growing inside me.

Silence is not the absence of God — it is the training ground of trust, where whispers become foundations.

But I've learned that God's "silence" is not the same as the silence we imagine. He is never truly quiet. He doesn't stop speaking; He simply refuses to conform to our demands for clarity on our terms. While I was straining to hear the answers I wanted, He was whispering the direction I needed. His silence is often His way of aligning me to His will and not mine. It is the unseen evidence that His timing is greater than my timetable.

I used to panic in the quiet. I mistook stillness for rejection. I mistook hiddenness for delay. I thought being overlooked meant I wasn't enough, or that I missed the moment. But now—I know better. Now I understand: silence is where I rise the deepest.

That's why it's so important for us to be healed from our trauma, our drama, our mistakes, and the wounds we've carried. If we don't allow God to heal those broken places, they will distort how we hear Him and how we interpret His movements. Unhealed hearts misread the silence. They assume God has abandoned them when He's actually protecting them. They interpret stillness as punishment when it's really preparation. That kind of misperception can be detrimental to our spirituality and faith, because it causes us to pull away from the very God who is drawing us closer.

Heaven does its best work in hushed places. In the still, He sharpens my hearing. In the concealed, He expands my capacity. In the unannounced, He strengthens my roots. I don't need to be broadcasted to be built. I don't need applause to carry anointing. The cocoon is proof: I can be wrapped in isolation and still be in divine motion.

And the Bible proves it. Joseph was forgotten in a prison cell, yet God was positioning him for a palace. David was anointed in a pasture long before he ever stepped on a battlefield. Even Jesus spent thirty years hidden in Nazareth before His public ministry began. Silence is not stagnation; it's God shaping you away from the crowd. What He does in obscurity will hold you steady in opportunity.

It's not that I don't have words. It's that the words God is giving me are too sacred to spill too early. Silence teaches stewardship. It tests what I'll say before the time. I'm not just quiet because I'm unsure—I'm quiet because I'm *being* sure. I'm becoming.

People often ask me where my depth comes from. My insight. My discernment. My fire. It didn't come from a microphone. It came from nights where God was my only audience. From mornings where my tears were the only conversation. From assignments I couldn't announce, but still had to carry. This silence? It's not weakness. It's weight.

This is where I learn not to retaliate. Not to prove. Not to respond to ignorance with impulse. This is where my integrity is purified. This is where my worship goes deeper than volume. And this is where my vision becomes precise. When the world is loud and the Spirit is still—I know I'm rising right.

I no longer resent the rooms I'm not invited to. I've learned to sit with the silence and watch the strategy form. The most dangerous version of me isn't the one that's visible. It's the one that's rooted in revelation, while the world thinks nothing is happening. That's when I'm hearing heaven the loudest.

She Rise in Silence means I trust God when there's no audience. I trust Him when there's no confirmation. I trust the process when there's no proof—yet. I know what's being built in me cannot be rushed, explained, or performed. It must be embodied. And embodiment requires stillness.

Because I don't just rise in celebration—I rise in consecration. I rise with my mouth closed and my spirit opened. I rise while questions are still swirling but obedience is steady. I rise in silence because that's where I'm sealed—sealed in strength, sealed in identity, sealed in the sound of His stillness.

And this is the part I want you to hear: silence is not a punishment; it's a promotion of trust. When you're tempted to rush out of the quiet, remember that even seeds sprout in the unseen. Your roots are reaching deeper than you realize. God is speaking, even when it feels like He is silent. His will is unfolding, even when your own timeline feels suspended.

Now go—rise in the stillness. Let your silence speak obedience. Let what God whispered form the foundation for what's coming next. You are not forgotten—you are being formed. Rise with ears to hear and roots that cannot be shaken.

She Rise, and the silence could not mute the sound of her faith.

"Stillness teaches you how to hold what tears will later release."

And when silence had done its work, when the soul had finally sat still long enough to hear its own name again...the tears came. Not just from sadness, but from release. From remembering. From letting go. What happens next in the rise is not quiet—but weeping. And not weakness—but washing.

She Rise While Weeping

"Weeping wasn't weakness—it was worship. And I cried until my memory remembered God."

Weeping has a language of its own. It speaks when words fail, it carries what the heart cannot articulate, and it reaches places prayers alone sometimes can't touch. Tears are not a sign of weakness — they are evidence of weight. The rise is never clean; it is soaked in nights of weeping that birth mornings of strength.

The Bible is full of weeping that turned into witness. Hannah's tears in the temple carried the cry of a barren woman — but God turned them into the birth of a prophet (1 Samuel 1). David's psalms are stained with tears that became songs, proving that worship is often born in weeping. Even Jesus Himself wept at Lazarus' tomb, though He knew resurrection was moments away (John 11:35). Scripture does not hide the tears; it honors them. Because in God's order, tears are not wasted — they are gathered (Psalm 56:8).

And I know this because I have lived it. There were nights when weeping was the only prayer I had. Nights when silence was broken only by sobs, and the rise seemed so far it felt like a lie. But I learned: weeping does not disqualify the rise — it prepares it. Weeping softens what pride hardens. Weeping clears out what bitterness tries to cement. Weeping humbles us into the kind of honesty God can actually use.

Tears don't mean I'm weak—they mean I'm still alive. Still tender. Still moving. I used to think weeping disqualified me from being strong, from being trusted, from being called. But I've learned that weeping doesn't cancel the rise—it accompanies it.

I rise while weeping because heaven never required perfection—only surrender. I came through life with a broken heart, long before I ever stood in a pulpit. I've walked through seasons where pain was my only companion and still kept moving forward. I've encouraged others with words I wasn't sure applied to me in the moment. I've smiled in rooms where I was still grieving the last place I left. And somehow, I've kept going—not because I had it all together, but because God held me together.

From Harlem to now, I've endured a season of great weeping. It wasn't just one moment—it was layer upon layer. Grief and loss of losing a parent. The ache of leaving behind an environment, a neighborhood, and the support system that shaped me. The people, the streets, the familiar rhythms of all I had known were suddenly no longer within reach. That kind of shifting is its own kind of grief. And when you're stripped of the places and people that once anchored you, the ground beneath your feet can feel fragile.

It wasn't just a physical move; it was a soul stretch—a stretch that included abandonment, emotional and mental abuse, betrayal, and a flood of uncertainty wrapped in lies. People who were supposed to cover me exposed me. People who said they loved me didn't know how to hold me without harming me. But I've lived through it—all of it. And I'm still here.

It has been my Joseph moment. What was meant for evil—what was born out of their own unhealed past, wounded filters, and fragile egos—God turned for my good (Genesis 50:20). I had to remember I don't wrestle against flesh and blood (Ephesians 6:12). I don't need to retaliate against broken people behaving from broken places. Some people hurt you not because they're evil—but because they're leaking from where they never healed, nor did they even know they needed healing. That doesn't excuse their actions, but it helps me remember the fight is not with them—it's with the wounds they never addressed. When you understand that, you stop handing your heart over to offense and start anchoring it in grace.

I could've mirrored their behavior, but I chose mercy instead. I could've built a wall, but I built a well. Not because it didn't hurt. But because I refused to let it harden me. And that's where true strength lies, not in your ability to clap back, but in your ability to stay soft enough for God to still pour through you.

And that's why healing matters so much. Unhealed hearts weaponize pain. They isolate when they need connection. They assume every loss is permanent when God is only pruning. I had to let God into the raw places. I had to surrender the bitterness and invite Him to turn my tears into intercession instead of anger. Because if I didn't, my grief would've consumed me, and I would've missed the glory that follows surrender.

Ultimately, your weeping is your vulnerability. And when it's brought before God without bitterness or wrath, it can lead to some of your greatest revelatory moments. Those tears soften the soil of your heart so wisdom can take root. They open you to see things you were too guarded to notice before. They position you to discern God's voice with fresh clarity because you're no longer pretending to be unshaken—you're honest, and heaven responds to honesty.

I feel the pain. But I find no fault. I've made peace with the fact that growth sometimes requires grief, and purpose often grows through pruning. Jesus wept at the tomb of Lazarus (John 11:35) even though He knew resurrection was coming. That shows me that tears don't contradict faith; they cleanse it. They don't disqualify me—they deepen me.

She Rise While Weeping is the testimony of the oil that flows from crushed places. It's what happens when I don't wait to feel strong to move forward. It's what happens when obedience meets agony, and destiny demands I show up—even while grieving what I can't explain. I've prayed with swollen eyes. I've prophesied through heartbreak. I've led when all I wanted was to be held. And yet—I rise.

This is not a story of pretending. This is not about faking strength. It's about sacred perseverance. It's about knowing that sometimes the rise happens in increments—inhale by inhale, tear by tear. Some days I walk upright. Some days I crawl forward. But I never stop.

People often see the fire in me and assume I've overcome everything. What they don't always see is that the fire was born in a furnace of sorrow. They see the mantle, but not the midnight cries. They hear the clarity in my voice, but they don't know how many tears it took to find it.

There is a kind of strength that doesn't roar—it leaks. Quiet. Consistent. Carried. That's the kind of strength I walk in now. I no longer wait for the pain to pass before I obey. I've learned to rise with tears running down my face and still say, "Yes, Lord."

I don't need a crowd to catch me. I just need God to carry me. And He always does. Psalm 56:8 says He bottles every tear, and I believe it. Even when I don't understand the cost. Even when I ache with unanswered questions. Even when I wonder if my rise is even seen—He sees it. He honors it.

"She doesn't wait until she stops weeping to rise. She doesn't wait until she's healed to help. She doesn't wait until the grief is over to release the glory within her. No, she rises right in the middle of it—because the call doesn't stop when the tears start. And because even in her sorrow, she knows she's still chosen."

This chapter of my life doesn't skip the weeping. It walks with it. And as I do, I'm learning to trust that every tear is counted. Every ache is shaping something eternal. And every rise—even while weeping—is a testimony in motion.

This is what it means to rise whole, even while healing.

Now go—rise through the ache. Let your tears testify. Let your grief grow gardens. You are not disqualified by your weeping—you are deepened by it. Obey through the tears, and glory will follow.

"Every tear watered the clarity you now carry.
Grief made you wise."

Grief became her wisdom. Tears became her training. What comes next in the rise is not collapse—but clarity. Not despair—but decision. Her tears were not in vain—they made room for strategy.

She Rise With Strategy

"I stopped apologizing for needing a plan. Survival taught me faith, but wisdom taught me how to build."

"She doesn't just rise with fire—she rises with form. With direction. With divine intelligence. With strategy written in scars. With rhythm shaped by the reality of suffering and the strength of survival."

Strategy is not always birthed in a boardroom. Sometimes it's born in broken rooms—rooms where you cried, rooms where you warred, rooms where you almost gave up. But what I've come to know is that God uses even those rooms as classrooms, teaching us to rise with insight we didn't know we carried. Strategy is the Spirit's way of converting your survival into your structure. It is how He takes what looked like weakness and turns it into wisdom.

I've learned that endless focus is on the points and not the problems. That is where breakthrough begins. Because when people dwell too long on the problems, they begin to weigh their pain against someone else's, trying to justify the state of their being. But healing doesn't come through comparison. Growth doesn't come from rehearsing wounds. Freedom is found in what we've learned, not just what we've lived. When we focus on the problems, we get stuck in cycles of defense and delay. But when we train ourselves to focus on the points—the revelation, the wisdom, the strategy, the strength—we move forward. There's no excuse why we can't find power in the midst of whatever we've gone through.

And this is especially true when it comes to trauma. Because when you have lived through seasons of trauma, you have to fight—and I mean really fight—not to become a person of drama. Trauma has triggers, and those triggers can pull you back into chaos if you aren't intentional. The enemy loves to nitpick in those places, just like the vultures that swarm an eagle. But an eagle knows how to rise above. And when you've come through trauma, you must learn to do the same: to get up on eagle's wings and fly above the drama.

This takes maturity. It takes discipline. It takes Spirit-led strategy. You have to decide not to be drawn into arguments, not to be baited by confrontations, not to fall into the chaos that people carry when they haven't yet healed. We live in a world that shouts "peace" but still thrives on conflict. People who are triggered by their own pain often look for a fight, a reason to be right, or a place to unload. And if you are not careful, your unhealed trauma will meet their unresolved drama—and suddenly, you're pulled out of position.

But strategy says: Don't take the bait. Strategy says: Stay on the wall. Keep your wings spread. Rise higher, don't sink lower. Because if the enemy can drag you into drama, he can shift your personality, your character, and even your heart. That's why you must be intentional, Spirit-led, and willing to rise above.

Strategy calls you to extract strength from what was sent to break you. It asks, what did I gain from the fire? What did I learn in the silence? What wisdom did I receive from the wilderness? These are the points. And the points are what you carry into your next level. The problems may have tried to define you, but the points will always refine you.

That's why strategy is never shallow. It is forged in fire, but it is sharpened in reflection. Strategy doesn't deny pain—it organizes it. It doesn't pretend storms didn't happen—it teaches you how to build an ark for the next one. Strategy is the Spirit's whisper: Use what you know. Apply what you've learned. Trust what I've shown you. And move as if I am with you—because I am.

Rising with strategy means you no longer respond out of impulse, but out of insight. It means you don't just shout, praise or worship in church—you build your life in a way that heaven can trust. It means your plans are not just yours; they are aligned with His will, tested by His Word, and empowered by His Spirit.

And so I rise with strategy. Not just emotion. Not just survival. Not just grit. But with the divine download that makes me more than a conqueror. Because when God gives you strategy, He gives you more than a step—He gives you a system. And systems break cycles.

And this is why strategy is not just personal—it is also biblical. The same way God teaches us in our broken rooms; He has always taught His people through His Word. Nehemiah set his heart to rebuild the walls of Jerusalem, and he did not only pray, but he also planned. He appointed families to specific gates, set watchmen on the walls, and divided labor so no section was left uncovered. Prayer birthed his strength, but strategy sustained his success (Nehemiah 4:13–18).

She rise with strategy because faith without works is still dead. Faith gives her vision, but strategy gives her movement. Faith tells her what is possible, but strategy teaches her what is next. If she rises without strategy, she may have zeal but no endurance, passion but no process, anointing but no alignment. Strategy takes what God whispers in prayer and organizes it into steps that keep her from collapsing under the weight of her own calling.

Strategy is also warfare. Esther did not run into the king's chamber the moment she discovered Haman's plot. She fasted. She waited. She invited the king to a banquet, then another. She built tension until the enemy exposed himself. That was strategy—patience positioned to protect her people (Esther 5–7). Strategy is knowing when to speak and when to stay silent, when to move and when to wait, when to release and when to restrain. It is not manipulation; it is wisdom moving in time with God.

Too many are losing because they mistake movement for momentum. But she rise with strategy. She studies her assignment, she discerns her timing, and she obeys her God. She does not waste her strength fighting battles she was never assigned, nor does she spend her nights trying to prove herself to people who were never meant to carry her mantle. She rise with strategy by counting the cost, by laying the foundation, and by building in such a way that even the enemy cannot easily dismantle what God has placed in her hands (Luke 14:28–30).

Strategy is her weapon against distraction. When others scatter, she builds. When others panic, she prays. When others seek shortcuts, she chooses the straight and narrow way. Strategy does not make her less spiritual—it makes her steward her spirituality with precision. Because anointing is powerful, but without strategy it can be poured out on the wrong soil.

She rise with strategy because she knows destiny is not stumbled into—it is stewarded.

And this is where strategy stops being theory and becomes my testimony. I don't just write about it—I live it. Strategy is not just what the Word confirms, it's what my life demands. And here's what I've learned in the living...

I no longer move just because I'm gifted—I move because I'm positioned. I don't just act on emotion—I act with intention. I use to fight to be understood. I use to try to explain my pain to people who preferred their own narratives. But I've learned: you can't build your future while trying to convince others of your truth. So, I stopped explaining and started executing. I don't argue—I fulfill.

People will always find ways to deny your pain to protect their own guilt. They will mislabel your survival to keep their narrative clean. When their world crumbles, they will blame you—not because you caused it, but because your growth made them uncomfortable. I've watched brokenness build itself around blame. And instead of staying stuck in the cycle of proving my innocence, I made a decision: move forward and don't look back.

Let them have the story. I have the strategy.

My strategy was born in quiet tears and violent prayers. It came from learning not just how to endure—but how to discern. How to walk away without becoming hard. How to recognize that sometimes the lesson isn't in the victory—it's in what didn't work. I've stopped being afraid to fail, because I now understand failures that are faced with faith become formulas for elevation.

I've learned that breakthrough begins with an endless focus on the points, not the problems. When people dwell too long on what went wrong, they start weighing their pain against someone else's—trying to justify the state of their being. But healing doesn't come through comparison. Growth doesn't come from rehearsing wounds. Freedom is found in what we've learned, not just what we've lived. Focusing on the problem traps us in cycles of defense and delay. But when we train our minds to focus on the points—the revelation, the wisdom, the strategy, the strength—we begin to move forward. There's no excuse not to find power in the midst of whatever we've gone through. So, at the age of twenty-two, I decided — and still decide today —I will no longer rehearse the story of my suffering just to prove I made it. I will extract the strength from it. I will collect the strategies. I will focus on the points. Because that's where the oil flows. That's where transformation lives.

So now I live by this rhythm:

- Pray. Praise. Live. Learn. Weep.
- Rename. Get up.
- Add to your strength. Throw away the sting.
- Rise again. Plan. Try. Pray.
- Succeed. Fail. Adjust.
- Jump and leap.
- Study. Learn. Apply.
- Nothing to prove.
- Something to live.
- Restore. Move.
- Don't settle.

This is not survival—this is strategy in motion. This is how I make it through the labyrinth. I don't waste time trying to be right. I waste no energy on *was*. I focus on *is*. I don't live to prove a point—I live to fulfill a prophecy.

Because strategy isn't noise—it's knowing. And my knowing is this: God is with me. And that's enough.

So when people ask how I keep rising, I don't hand them my tears—I show them my fruit. The fruit of obedience. The fruit of longevity. The fruit of having chosen healing when bitterness was easier. The fruit of grace under pressure and power under fire.

"She Rise with strategy because she's no longer navigating with survival instincts—she's moving with kingdom intelligence and divine strategy. She's mapping out healing for others through the wounds she refused to worship. She's designing wholeness for those who once misunderstood her silence. She's not just trying—she's triumphing through tools."

Because now, I don't just carry oil—I carry order. I'm not just gifted—I'm governed.

And the fruit will speak.

Because her rise is no longer reactive—it's refined.

Now go—rise with precision. Let your scars speak strategy. Let your discernment lead the way. Govern what you've been given. Move like oil with order. The fruit will not lie.

"The plan was never just about escape. It was about formation."

Every strategy is tested. What you write down must be walked out. And before the promise comes to pass, the storm often comes to press. But not every storm destroys—some storms form. And just like a snowflake, her rise is shaped in the atmosphere of adversity. Here, she becomes.

She Rise: From Storm to Endurance, Formed Like a Snowflake

"Not every storm is sent to break you. Some are sent to sculpt you—layer by sacred layer."

My name is Sherrise. And whether they know it or not, it means She Rise. Not "she rose" as in a moment that already passed. Not "she will rise" as in a future that still tarries. But She Rise. Present tense. Ongoing. Perpetual. It is not just a name—it's a mandate. And that mandate has moved me through many seasons, each marked by a name Heaven authored.

Storm is an identity. Not a label of chaos, but a mantle of strength. Storm is not easily dismissed—it demands attention, it shifts atmospheres, and it makes way for change. Storm is not sent to ruin, but to wake things up. To reveal what is hidden. To stir what has grown stagnant. And just as God has used storms to part seas, to cleanse the earth, and to answer out of whirlwinds, Storm is a name He still gives. Not destruction—but preparation. Not ruin—but renewal.

Our perspective must change. It is not based on what we feel about a thing—for Storm is not derogatory. It is the outcome that produces heaven's will that matters most. When our perception shifts, we begin to see that even in the things we once called negative, we can trace the handiwork of God. And that sight becomes the very degree by which we pull for strength. There will never be a heaven decision that makes earthly sense. And when I discovered that, it was not an easy adjustment—but I have learned to have sight beyond sight.

> *"Storm is not the force that destroys.*
> *Storm is the strength that clears the air,*
> *waters the ground,*
> *and makes way for new growth."*

Storm was the mantle God revealed—strength in motion, atmosphere shifting, change announcing. But endurance was the life I was called to live. That's when the name iEndure came. I didn't earn it—I became it. I endured more than people knew. I survived what should've sealed me. I outlasted what was sent to silence me. Endurance became my identity because it was what God required of me when strength had no script and hope had no words. iEndure isn't just what I say—it's who I am. It's what I carry when the lights are off, the room is silent, and the process feels never-ending. I endure, not because I'm invincible, but because I'm anchored in the invisible.

And then—when all was still—God whispered something delicate but deliberate. In a moment of sacred quietness, He called me 'Snowflake'. It wasn't a name from mockery—it was a name from Majesty. Or maybe not a name at all—but an identity. A posture. A way He showed me how I was shaped. He said it not because I was fragile, but because I was formed uniquely. No two snowflakes are alike. They fall quietly from the heights. They are crafted in cold, in silence, in softness. And yet—when seen up close—their beauty is unmatched, their pattern is mathematical perfection, and their descent is divinely timed. That name was God's way of affirming that I wasn't created to fit in. I was created to fall from glory and land with purpose.

So here I am. Sherrise. She Rise. The one who was once Storm. The one who became iEndure. The one whispered to as Snowflake. These are not contradictions. They are confirmations. Layers of my calling. Storm gave me my roar. iEndure gave me my root. Snowflake gave me my reason. And all of them live beneath the name that will never be stolen from me: She Rise.

Even when I don't know how to name the season I'm in—I know who I am within it. I am navigating not just with survival in mind, but with strategy in motion. I am not stuck. I am not random. I am becoming. And every storm I've weathered, every silence I've survived, every name I've carried has been evidence that my rise is not performance—it's prophecy.

A dear friend once said, "You are the instructions navigating through the storm." And I believe it. Because I'm not just telling people how to overcome—I'm walking out the manual in real time. I am the living scroll. The moving revelation. The handwritten strategy with tear-streaked ink and heaven-breathed fire.

So yes, I rise. But not just in public. I rise in silence. I rise in storms. I rise in snow. I rise when no one sees, and I rise when Heaven says go. My name holds it all.

Sherrise. She Rise.

Now go—rise with your name in alignment. Let every storm refine you. Let every tear mark your trail. Let every whisper from God redefine what strength looks like. You are not scattered—you are sacredly shaped. Walk in the pattern He formed. Rise like only you can.

"The storm didn't just pass—it passed through her. And she lived."

She came through what should've ended her. The storm didn't just test her—it transformed her. And now, after all the winds and waves, she emerges not broken but healed. Not lost, but whole.

She Rise Healed

"Healing isn't hiding. It's living like the wound no longer owns you."

Before I could rise, I had to heal. And healing wasn't pretty. It wasn't quick. It wasn't even what I expected. Healing meant walking through seasons I never asked for, carrying weights I didn't see coming, and learning to trust God in places I never planned to be. It meant moving through changes, transitions, and trials that shaped me in ways comfort never could. But it was in healing that I discovered power—not the power of pretending, but the power of becoming.

Healing taught me that obstacles don't mean you're broken beyond repair—they mean you're being refined. It taught me that every move, every loss, every unexpected turn was not punishment, but preparation. Healing was not about me being difficult, it was about me being developed. God was not exposing me to shame; He was positioning me for strength.

And so, I tell my story not from the posture of pity, but from the position of power. Not to bring attention to pain, but to make space for truth. Not to relive what broke me, but to remind you that brokenness isn't the end—it's the place where

God begins again. I told you my story because I don't want you to be ashamed of yours. This isn't about broadcasting everything you've been through. It's about no longer hiding the beauty of how far you've come.

You don't have to explain what happened. You don't have to relive it to prove you've survived it. But you do have to recognize it. You do have to confront it—not for punishment, but for peace. You do have to own it—not to wear it as a label, but to strip it of its power. Silence does not heal. And denial doesn't erase. We heal by truth. By confrontation. By letting God walk us back through what tried to bury us and letting Him resurrect what was never meant to die in us.

The world is broken because healing has been neglected. People keep repeating what hurt them. They fight to be right, instead of being made whole. They relive wounds instead of releasing them. They wait for apologies that may never come and miss the permission to heal anyway.

We stay trapped in cycles because no one taught us how to break them. But I'm telling you now: you can break it.

You can rise healed.
You can rise whole.
You can rise holy.
You can rise human.

You can rise honest.

You don't have to list what happened. You don't have to justify your journey. You just have to make the decision to rise—above every rejection, every betrayal, every diagnosis, every silent season that told you healing was too far away.

You have to rise above:

- Every voice that silenced yours.
- Every lie that said you were too broken.
- Every moment that made you feel disposable.
- Every delay that made you question your worth.

This chapter isn't a testimony of perfection. It's the testament of a decision—To not let trauma be the final author of your life. To not let pain define your pace. To not let shame rob you of your shape.

Healing is not a one-time cry—it's a lifestyle of choosing to live again, every single day. I had to learn that healing wasn't loud—it didn't always come in fire or flashes of revelation. Sometimes it whispered. Sometimes it looked like me getting up without needing to explain. Sometimes it looked like tears that no longer hurt, just the soul releasing what it had already survived. Sometimes it looked like saying, "No more" and meaning it. Sometimes it meant closing doors I didn't get closure from.

I realized I didn't need to win arguments to walk in peace.

I didn't need a crowd to confirm my healing.

I didn't need a full understanding of why—it was enough to know Who.

God healed me in stages. Quiet ones. Private ones. Sometimes in worship. Sometimes in confrontation. Sometimes while folding laundry and whispering scriptures over myself. He didn't rush me—but He refused to leave me undone.

You are not crazy for needing time.

You are not weak for needing help.

You are not broken beyond repair.

And even when others weaponized their instability against me, I chose peace. I chose not to match dysfunction, but to manage my healing. I no longer explain their behavior—I protect my boundaries.

And while you wait on some things to change, become the changed one. Be the healed one. Be the interrupter of generational silence. Be the proof that God still resurrects stories and breathes life into forgotten places.

You are not what happened to you.

You are what God has redeemed you to be.

So, forgive.

Forgive as quickly as possible.

I didn't say reconcile; Forgive.

Forgive so you can move.

Forgive so you can build again.

Forgive so your dreams don't carry the scent of decay.

Forgive so your children don't have to heal from what you refused to face.

You were never meant to stay in survival mode. You were meant to build, flourish, and pour from a healed vessel.

This is not the chapter of shame. This is the chapter of shifting. The day when pain stops being your compass, and peace takes the lead.

Declare this over your life:
- I am not my wound.
- I am the healing that came from it.
- I am not the battle.
- I am the breakthrough.
- I am not just surviving.
- I am whole. I am rising. I am healed.

- So, Rise.
- Rise without apology.
- Rise without residue.
- Rise without needing them to understand.
- Rise without carrying guilt that doesn't belong to you.
- Rise with grace. Rise with grit.
- Rise, healed.
- Let your healing be louder than their opinion.
- Let your healing outshine your history.
- Let your healing glorify God in a way that
- nothing else could.
- This chapter ends the cycle.
- This chapter begins the becoming.
- This chapter declares what hell couldn't stop:
- She Rise…Healed.

Healing is not a theory. It's a posture. It's not just something we talk about—it's something we live out. And yet, in this generation, we often rehearse healing while still living like we're wounded. We say the right words but display the wrong posture. We profess healing, but our patterns still submit to pain.

True healing doesn't need constant justification. It doesn't ask for a platform to prove it. Healed women—and healed men—go tell and show what the Lord has done. Like the one leper who returned to give thanks, healed people carry a witness that doesn't demand attention but commands it through transformation.

The moment we start trying to *reason* ourselves into healing, we begin to dilute it. Healing is not logic—it's liberation. It's obedience. It's quiet trust. It's strategy. It's walking like the woman who touched the hem and knew she was made whole, even when the crowd still remembered her crawl.

We've built taglines that excuse the absence of true deliverance. We say things like, "Healing is a journey" but use it to justify staying stuck. Healing is a journey, yes—but a journey moves. Healing is not a holding cell. It is the open gate. And too many have confused delay with discipleship. But if you're still trying to prove your pain, then you're not walking in your healing.

Real healing makes us responsible. It makes us stewards. It gives us the power to live again—but not recklessly. We don't return to old environments in the name of proving 'we're fine'. Healed does not mean paranoid. Healed means wise. Healed means I forgive because carrying that weight is too heavy for the assignment ahead. Healed means I learn how to manage the sensations of what once was. Like arthritis flaring in the rain—I recognize the signal, I apply the treatment, but I don't cancel my day.

Healing may leave a scar, a limp, or a memory—but it doesn't leave us paralyzed. It teaches us how to walk with awareness, not fear. How to plan with faith, not fantasy. Healing doesn't glorify pain—it glorifies God in spite of it.

So don't neglect your healing trying to prove your history. Don't water down your deliverance trying to relate to where you no longer belong. Deal with the wound, acknowledge the weather, but let your rising be louder than your reasoning.

Healed is not a place of denial. It's a place of dominion.

Healed is not always loud—but it's always evident.

Healed is not being pain-free. It's being spirit-led, even in the moments when pain tries to speak.

You are healed because there is more.

You are healed to rise.

You are healed to build.

You are healed to live.

Healing is not about forgetting. It's about growing. It's about managing the miracle wisely. The evidence of healing isn't just absence of pain—it's the presence of forward movement.

Because She Rise healed.

Now go—rise as the healed one. Let peace be your posture. Let wisdom be your rhythm. Don't just carry your healing—walk it out with clarity, responsibility, and grace.

Let them see the glory on your scars, not the sting of your wounds. You are the living evidence: God heals for purpose.

"Not every rising is loud. Some resurrections happen in silence, some breakthroughs bloom in the dark. But all transformation leaves evidence—even when no one saw it happen."

Before the wings ever opened, before the flight ever came, there was breaking, stretching, morphing. This next rise is not about applause—it's about truth. Not about image—it's about substance. The next pages are for the ones who transformed quietly, faithfully, and sometimes painfully—without ever needing to be seen. The ones who followed the light without asking for a spotlight. This is your honoring. This is your emergence.

She Rise in Morph: Honoring the Hidden Transformations

"Transformation isn't always glamorous—but it is always glorious."

They always tell the story of the butterfly.

They teach us to look for beauty with open wings, vibrant colors, and effortless flight. But what of the ones who rise with none of that sparkle? What of the ones who still went through the dark, still endured the crushing cocoon, but didn't come out with the applause of the world—just the presence of perseverance?

What of the moth, who morphs just like the butterfly, but is rarely noticed, rarely celebrated, rarely seen as divine?

We've romanticized the butterfly and overlooked the sacred mystery of the moth. But she morphs too. She too spins her cocoon. She too breaks herself open. She too transforms. But she does so in the dark. She emerges at night. She flies by faith, not by fanfare. And maybe that's exactly why her transformation is holier.

The butterfly announces spring, but the moth endures the night.

There is something sacred about not needing to be seen to know you've changed. About flying without the world's validation. About finding your way to the light with no roadmap—just the instinct of a spirit reborn. Moths don't chase attention. They follow light. They are not here to please; they are here to be drawn—to the Source, to the Stillness, to the Signal that only the Spirit gives.

I sat on a balcony once, and a large moth came to me, largest I've ever seen. Not just flying by—but circling, as if to say, "You are being watched. You are being witnessed. You are being welcomed into a deeper understanding of your process." And then it laid there. Not in fear. Not in haste. It rested as if to say, "We who morph in silence also deserve to be still."

And I heard it in my spirit: Transformation is not always glamorous, but it is always glorious.

To those who feel like their metamorphosis doesn't match the pictures in the books, I say: You are still rising.

To those whose beauty is not in boldness, but in endurance, I celebrate you.

To the one who has grown in the dark and never told a soul how long it took to break free, I see you.

To the one who is still morphing, still hiding, still waiting for their wings to be understood, I call you beautiful.

This is the celebration of the unsung emergence.

The unflashy victory.

The moth-made miracle.

Because not all transformations are meant to be loud. Some are meant to be true.

So rise, whether your wings look like fire or fabric, sparkle or softness. Just rise.

Moth or butterfly—you changed. You broke through. You are flying.

And that's enough.

Truth is, no matter how many times you've been dropped, most people can't see it on the outside. The scars don't always show up on the surface right away. But beneath the skin, something begins to shift—sometimes break, sometimes swell, sometimes calcify. And if you're not careful, what was once hidden beneath the surface will start to manifest in bruises your spirit can't conceal.

So, you must pause.

You must examine yourself.

Not casually. Not vaguely.

But thoroughly.

Because after you've been dropped, you're injured.

And when you keep pretending like you're not, when you keep functioning over fractures and dressing up your limp like it's a walk of confidence, you begin living, speaking, and manifesting injuries in ways you haven't even recognized.

You start bleeding into your relationships.

You start stiffening in your prayer life.

You start limping in your discipline.

And soon, what you didn't examine becomes the very thing that holds you back from the maturity you claim you want.

Every drop.

Every disappointment.

Every betrayal.

Every delayed promise.

Every subtle dismissal.

It must be examined.

Not just spiritually.

But mentally.

Emotionally.

Physically.

Socially.

Even financially.

Because the Body cannot grow lighter if the members keep ignoring their injuries.

And you cannot rise trustworthy if you keep skipping over the places where you've fallen.

Just because you're still moving doesn't mean you're not wounded.

And moving in a wounded spirit is one of the easiest ways to disguise immaturity as strength.

But you don't have to live disguised.

You can be healed.

You can be rebuilt.

You cannot carry a spirit that only a mother could love.

You cannot keep walking in a character that must always be explained, excused, or endured by those who know you best. That kind of spirit won't carry weight in Kingdom places. That kind of character cannot be trusted with assignment. If you want to rise transformed, you'll have to allow the Spirit of God to take you through a blood-deep identity reset—back to the One whose blood didn't just cleanse you, but re-coded you.

This rise is not about proving you are still lovable.

It's about becoming someone who is trustworthy, tested, and tried and still comes out holy.

It's about producing the kind of fruit that shows up in rooms where no one knows your name, but they know His Spirit.

It's about becoming credible in the courts of Heaven and usable in the earth.

Ask yourself honestly: Have you been leaning too long on the kind of love that coddles instead of the kind of love that crucifies?

Because maternal love will wrap you, but divine love will rework you.

Maternal love says, "You're still my baby," while divine love says, "Behold, you are Mine, now rise." I didn't know this kind of love as a daughter. I stopped being a daughter in the way most understand it after the age of ten. Love couldn't hold me so God healed me enough to hold others without passing down the hurt I had to survive. I understand that most of it was not intentional, and I speak from a healed place, but that doesn't erase the reality of the damage that emotionally unhealed dysfunction can cause. I became something else. A survivor. A protector. A provider. And I learned quickly that when people have not healed, the love they offer can wound you. I had to figure out how to parent without a pattern, how to love without a blueprint. And what I discovered is that while I didn't learn love through being held, I found its truest meaning in having to hold others through pain, through growth, through their own wilderness moments.

I didn't learn love through the scope of being nurtured—I learned it through necessity. As I grew older, I had to stretch to become the kind of mother who didn't just comfort but commissioned. The kind of parent who didn't just shield, but shaped. Who didn't just say, "Come lay down," but said, "Come lay down and let me speak life into your dry places while I show you the way forward."

I couldn't love through the scope of my longing, or I would have damaged them. I had to love them beyond my ache. Beyond what I didn't get. Beyond what I didn't feel. And somehow, in giving them what I never had, I started to see love rightly.

It wasn't just sweet and soothing—it was sacrificial and forming. Love that spoke life and gave direction, not just comfort. Love that looked in their eyes and said, "I know it's hard, but I see the power in you. I see the mantle on your life. I know what you carry, and I refuse to let you settle here." Love that didn't excuse everything but expected something. Not with a love that hovers over their pain… but with a love that holds them accountable to their purpose. Not because I wanted to control them, but because I saw God's image in them.

I wasn't trying to raise children who could just function with me, I was raising children who could function without me and thrive wherever God sent them. But I had to be careful. I couldn't project my voids onto their victories. I couldn't love them through the lens of my own longing, or I would have damaged them. I had to love them beyond my need for emotional repayment.

Because the pattern we don't confront will quietly embed itself into our legacy. And what we don't fix… they will feel. Unspoken, but inherited. Invisible, but impactful.

So, I had to love them from a surrendered place—a place that said, "I may not have received it, but I will become it."

Becoming that kind of mother revealed something about God I never saw before.

It wasn't soft-only love. It wasn't all-affirming and always soothing. It was love with clarity. Love with weight. Love with expectation. Love that confronts, shapes, equips, protects, and releases.

And that kind of love… that weighty, wise, war-tested love? That's how God loves me. That's why I can endure hard doctrine like a soldier. That's why correction doesn't break me—it builds me. That's why I don't flinch when God challenges me. I've learned that true love doesn't coddle my dysfunction. It prepares me for destiny.

Motherhood morphed me. It taught me how to speak resurrection even when I wanted to be silent. It taught me that sometimes your nurturing is the nourishment—but other times, it's your no that becomes the next lesson. And I wasn't just raising them—I was being raised too. I was being raised into the kind of woman who didn't just say, "I'm here if you fall," but also said, "I'm here to make sure you fly."

That's when I understood what divine love truly is.

It's not passive. It's not permissive. It's prophetic.

It sees where you're going—even when you can't. And because I loved them, I had to say things I didn't want to say. Because I loved them, I had to lead even when I wanted to disappear. Because I loved them, I had to let them break through instead of breaking down.

This is the kind of love that morphs us all.

Because what God births through you will stretch you.

And what you birth in obedience will teach you how God feels about you, too.

So no, I didn't know this from a mother to a child. But I learned it as a mother to my children. And the lesson keeps unfolding.

So, rise.

Rise from immature emotionalism into anchored identity.

Rise from the kind of neediness that drains others, into the kind of wholeness that blesses them.

Rise from entitlement into entrusted maturity.

Because being loved is not the same as being ready.

The truth is many try to walk in purpose, with a spirit still stuck in approval addiction. Wanting applause before developing the kind of character that deserves audience. Craving platforms without ever proving the strength to stand firm in hidden places.

But hear this:

Love that doesn't correct you is counterfeit.

And rising that doesn't transform you is just performance.

You will need to be re-fathered by God.

Not just healed—but re-coded.

Not just accepted—but realigned.

Not just understood—but uprooted.

You do not need the familiar to prove your worth.

You've been loved too deeply to stay untrustworthy.

Now rise—fruitful.

Rise clean.

Rise re-identified.

Because She Rise when the Father rewrites the spirit to reflect His Son.

She Rise trustworthy.

She Rise beyond what only a mother could love.

She Rise to be used—not just known.

She Rise from being carried to being called.

She Rise—and her fruit remains.

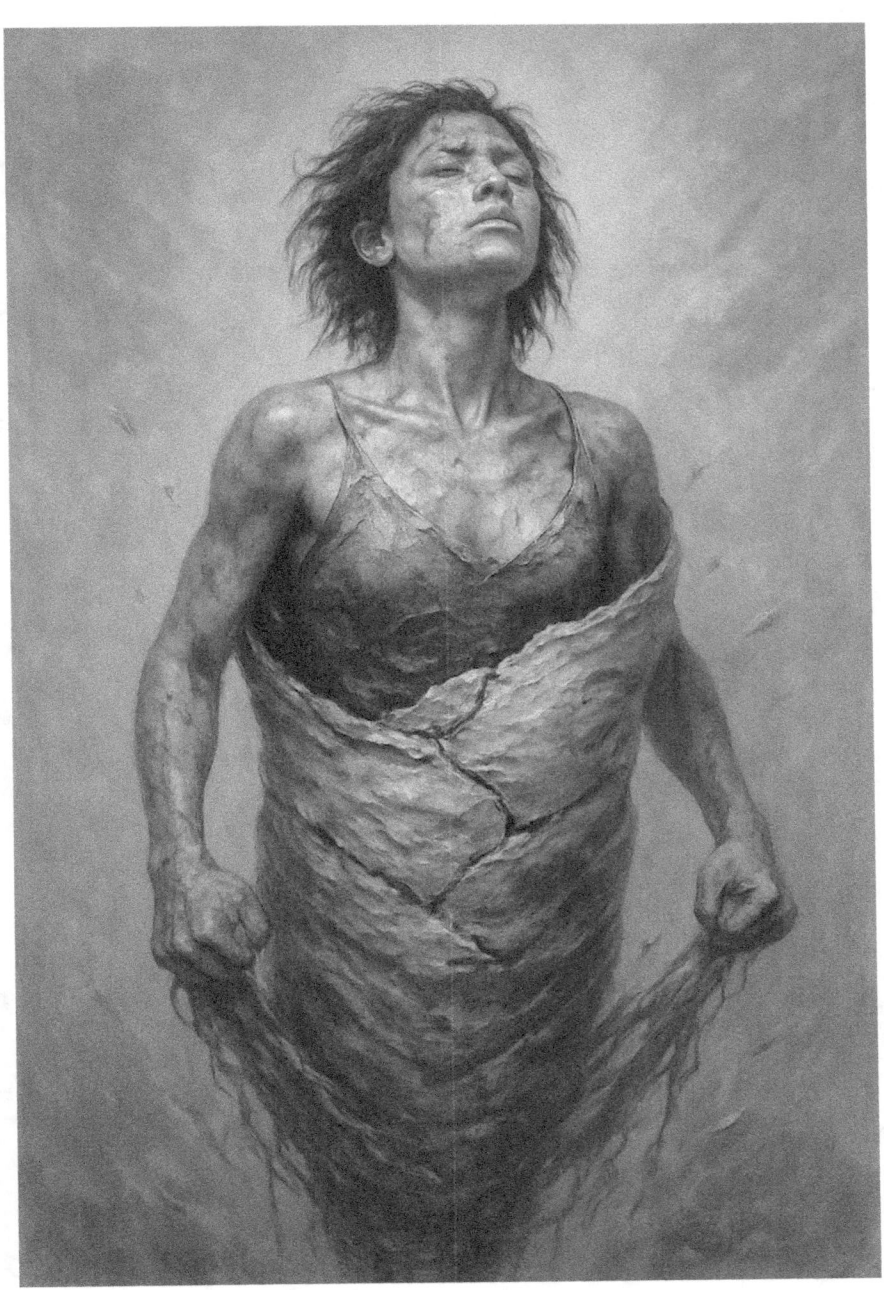

"Healing made her light enough to run again. So she ran...past statistics, past shame, past fear."

Healing isn't the end—it's the beginning of proving what you've overcome. And just when the enemy thought she wouldn't make it, she rose up again. Healed and whole—and unstoppable. She didn't just survive. She defeated every odd.

Because She Rise, She Defeated the Odds

"The odds never had a chance—because I wasn't betting on myself. I was standing in covenant."

I wasn't supposed to make it—not with what I've lived through. Not with the silence I carried, the sorrow I survived, or the systems I was born into. If you looked at the odds—the statistics, the trauma, the betrayals, the generational patterns you'd expect someone else. Someone stuck. Someone broken. Someone bitter. But instead, you have me. Standing. Whole. Becoming. Teaching. Rising.

Because She Rise, the odds lost their grip.

I didn't just beat the odds, I redefined what was even possible. Not because I was stronger, but because I surrendered deeper. Because I allowed God to rewrite the story while I was still bleeding. Because I didn't wait for the pain to pass—I rose in it. I rose from Harlem to here. From rejection to resilience. From abandonment to authority. From being the one who was discarded, to the one who now declares.

Let the record show: the trauma didn't finish me. The betrayal didn't own me. The lies didn't label me. And the fear didn't frame me. Every tear that tried to drown me, became the river God used to carry me into destiny. Every closed door became a redirect into something holy. I rise, not in spite of the odds, but as the proof that they don't get the final word. I didn't grow up in privilege; I didn't rise on the wings of ease. My journey came with misunderstanding, survival, isolation, and invisible war. But still—She Rise. I rose through unspoken grief and unanswered questions. I rose with people walking away and others trying to copy what they never endured. They mimicked the fruit but never met the fire. They tried to wear what cost me everything, not realizing that oil doesn't flow from imitation—it flows from intimacy. This isn't about superiority—it's about stewardship. The anointing was forged in obedience, not borrowed through association.

What they called "too much" became the evidence I carried more than they could see. What they overlooked, is what God anointed. What they tried to break in me, only revealed how unbreakable I am in Him.

And here's the truth they never expected:
Because She Rise, the family now has a remnant.
Because She Rise, the silence has a sound.
Because She Rise, the next generation has a path.

Because She Rise, the altar still has fire.

Because She Rise, legacy has language. Because She Rise, what was once scattered is now covered. And Because She Rise, you rise too—she is me, and she is YOU!

I know what it feels like to carry destiny while dodging destruction. I know what it means to rise with shaking knees, exhausted eyes, and no one clapping for you but heaven. But I also know what it means to win quietly. To walk in rooms, I was never supposed to enter. To carry revelation, I didn't learn—I lived. To speak with oil drawn from the press no one knew I was under.

I am not just healed—I'm happening.

I'm not just a survivor—I'm a seed sower, system breaker, and cycle shifter.

And the odds? They're broken.

Not because I avoided pain.

But because I obeyed God in it.

If I had avoided the pain, I would have avoided the power. If I had chosen silence, I would have forfeited sound. If I had hidden from the battle, I would have missed the blessing. If I had given up, destiny would have dried up. But I didn't. I obeyed, I endured, and I rose.

Getting into a race you know is already won is something we should all do if we truly trust the God we serve. Defeating the odds stacked against us isn't just about our fight, it's about our faith. And sometimes it's not even a conscious awareness. You just keep going. You keep showing up. You endure. And before you know it, victory becomes inevitable, in spite of it all.

She Rise—and because of that, hell lost its bet. The odds are not just beaten—they are defeated. Their grip is gone. Their voice is silenced. And their power to predict my future has been permanently revoked by the One who holds it.

Now go—rise like the remnant. Let obedience speak louder than odds. Let your becoming interrupt every statistic. Let your rising confirm what trauma couldn't cancel. You are not the exception—you are the evidence. Hell bet on her silence, but she rose speaking. Hell bet on her breaking, but she rose building. Hell bet on her death in it, but she rose living through it. And because she rose, hell lost its bet forever. So walk like silence has already been shattered. Walk like every odd has already been overturned. Walk like the bet is broken—because it is.

"Victory is not an ending. It's a signal to build."

The war is over, but the work begins. Victory gave her breath, but purpose gave her tools. And now, she doesn't just testify, she builds. With wisdom. With strength. With oil.

She Rise: The Anatomy of My Becoming

"Becoming is not about becoming someone new—it's about recovering every part of who you were always meant to be."

Before the spotlight. Before the sound. Before the structure of ministry, there was the silence of formation. This chapter isn't a detour from the message—it is the message. The becoming is part of the rising. What you read here isn't the story of a woman trying to be 'deep'. It's the story of a vessel being designed. These aren't just memories—they're markers. This is what it looks like when God forms someone from the inside out.

My journey isn't random, it's prophetic. I am rooted in an Ezekiel vision. I see through wheels, realms, and resurrection. I carry a Moses mandate, birthing deliverance while battling doubt. I embody Paul's resilience—scarred but sent, shipwrecked but still speaking. And I echo Job's faith—misunderstood and sifted but never severed from God's sovereignty.

This combination vision, mandate, resilience, and faith isn't just a spiritual résumé. It's the anatomy of my becoming. I've wept through the weight of it, but I no longer apologize for how deeply I feel the fire, or how intentionally I chase the cloud. I'm not here for performance; I'm here for presence. I'm not called to imitate; I'm called to ignite. And so, I say to myself in this evolving chapter: Keep walking. Keep watching. Keep waiting. The cocoon is not the end. It's where wings are written into your DNA.

This season is stretching me, but it's also speaking to me. And what it's saying is this: I was never made for comfort—I was made for glory. I breathe deeply. I surrender daily. I write prophetically. I live with fire in my bones—even when no one sees the flame. Because I'm not just surviving storms—I'm becoming the strategy others will need to rise through their own.

There's a reason things don't come easy for me. I used to wonder why every door felt heavier, every process longer, every season more layered than the last. But I understand now—this isn't punishment, it's preparation. I haven't just been called to transition—I've been called to transformation. That means I don't just go through things—I become something because of them.

My call is apostolic-prophetic—so yes, it's heavy. It stretches through realms, reforms systems, and unlocks deliverance in places most people never see. But yours might be different. Maybe your becoming is maternal. Or marketplace. Or musical. Or healing. That doesn't make it any less divine. The process may vary, but the consecration is always sacred. Whatever your shape—trust it. Heaven carved it for a reason.

More and more, I see my life as a divine cocoon. Not just confined—but concealed for consecration. This isn't about delay for the sake of pain. It's about divine development. Delayed gratification isn't just a test—it's a blueprint for trust. I'm being prepared to fly in ways I've never seen before—but first, my wings must be formed in silence.

I carry a settled truth that I've mentioned earlier that emerged as a word from a friend but now stands as a mantle across every part of my life: "You are the instructions navigating through the storm." Not just a phrase for encouragement—it's the framework of how I move, minister, and multiply what God has given me. I don't just walk through adversity—I am the strategy within it. I've learned to recognize it in my leadership, in my silence, in my survival, in my creativity, and in my counsel. What began as confirmation has now become construction—I build with it. I teach from it. I carry it. And I no longer wonder why I'm wired this way. I understand that what I've lived was never just personal—it's purposeful. I am the evidence and the example, not for applause, but for assignment.

Because She Rise, she doesn't just carry the fire—she carries the frame.

Becoming is not about elevation; it's about formation. What God forms in you will sustain what He entrusts to you. And the battle over your identity is the battle over your destiny. If the enemy can distort how, you see yourself, he can delay who you are becoming.

Identity is the first alignment. Without it, everything else feels like reaching for air. Jesus knew this. Before He ever worked a miracle, the Father's voice anchored Him: "This is my beloved Son, in whom I am well pleased." And almost immediately, the enemy tried to unseat that identity in the wilderness: "If thou be the Son of God…" The enemy attacks who you are, before he ever touches what you're called to do. Because if you don't know who you are, you will chase validation instead of walking in Kingdom alignment.

The lies have to be silenced—those whispers of not enough, too much, too broken, too late. Identity is not fragile. It was formed before time began: "Before I formed thee in the belly I knew thee." God knew you. He set you apart long before applause or assignment. And if your worth is unsettled, your authority will always be under attack. *Becoming* demands that identity and authority walk together.

Once identity is secured, the call is to become a student of the Father. Not just a servant following orders, but one who lingers in His presence, learning His ways. "Wisdom is the principal thing… and with all thy getting get understanding." This posture keeps you from mistaking busyness for obedience. It protects you from drifting into routine, moving without His voice. Jesus modeled this: "The Son can do nothing of himself, but what he seeth the Father do." That is the anatomy of a student. That is the anatomy of becoming.

But the classroom isn't enough if there's no movement. What you learn must translate into how you live. Abraham showed this when he obeyed and went out, "not knowing whither he went." That is obedience in motion—trusting the unseen more than the visible.

Obedience will stretch you. It will test you. There will be Gethsemane moments when you whisper Jesus' words: "Not my will, but thine, be done." Because delayed obedience is still disobedience. Partial obedience is still disobedience. And selective obedience will always block the fullness of what God wants to do.

Even obedience leads into fire—the refining fire. There are seasons that strip away false strength, seasons that feel like punishment but are really preparation: "He shall sit as a refiner and purifier of silver."

Refining hurts. It isolates. It exposes. Yet it is the only place where pride is burned away, and purity is born. It's where God makes you a vessel capable of carrying His glory without cracking. "The trial of your faith…though it be tried with fire, might be found unto praise and honour and glory."

The fruit of refining is endurance and maturity; a life anchored in His timing: "Afterward it yieldeth the peaceable fruit of righteousness." Refining makes you unshakeable.

And only then can there be release. But release is not promotion—it is stewardship. Can you handle what He places in your hand with faithfulness? Will you see your gifts, your platform, your influence as possessions or assignments?

When clutching stops, carrying begins. And it can be carried well because it was never about self. "It is required in stewards, that a man be found faithful." Faithful when no one is watching. Faithful when it feels like too little. Faithful when called forward, and faithful when asked to wait.

This is the culmination of becoming. No longer striving to build something personal. No longer chasing validation. A steward of the Father's heart, a carrier of His Kingdom.

This is the rhythm He's been writing all along, and it's the rhythm He's writing in you. Don't despise your silence; it's building strategy. Don't curse your fire; it's forming purity. Don't resent your process; it's producing a prototype.

What you've survived wasn't just for testimony—it was for teaching. Don't just rise transformed—rise transferable. Because She Rise, she doesn't just carry the fire—she carries the frame. And you, too, are becoming the blueprint.

Now go—rise with awareness. Let your silence build strategy. Let your process become the prototype. What you've survived wasn't just for testimony—it was for teaching. Don't just rise transformed—rise transferable. You are becoming the blueprint.

"Becoming shapes the vessel; tools steward the treasure it carries."

The anatomy of my becoming revealed the layers of who I am, but identity without equipping is incomplete. Becoming gives me the posture; tools give me the reach. They turn revelation into action, strength into strategy, and survival into stewardship. Now, I step forward not just as one who has been formed, but as one prepared to build.

She Rise with Tools

"The oil taught me how to use the tools. I don't just survive anymore—I steward."

There was no handbook for the kind of rising I had to do. No blueprint for how to make it out when your world is crumbling but your spirit refuses to stay buried. I had to gather tools—not just things, but truths. Songs, scriptures, prayers, and a quiet kind of resilience became my weaponry. And not the kind you wield to hurt, but the kind you carry to build.

This chapter is not a performance—it's a toolbox. A lived-through revelation. I didn't just survive pain; I studied it. I dissected the reasons behind the silence, the tension, the warfare. I tracked the trail of abandonment. betrayal and discovered patterns. I didn't just cry through it. I learned through it. I rose with information, with wisdom, with Holy Spirit insight.

I embraced every encounter, not for its permanence, but for its purpose.

I rise because I understand now that stagnation is just as dangerous as bitterness. It keeps you rehearsing instead of rebuilding. It makes you question instead of conquer. But once

I trusted God's way and not my own timing, I learned that tools show up as people, as moments, as scriptures, as sounds.

One of those tools was a song by Lalah Hathaway, "So They Say". In it, she sings about how time heals all wounds. But I didn't just wait for time. I made use of the time. I cried in it. I processed in it. I prayed and built and broke and rose in it. That song was a mirror—it gave voice to places I hadn't yet verbalized. It helped me trust that the process wasn't punishment—it was placement.

My life became a toolbox. Galatians 2:20 became a foundational reminder—I am crucified with Christ, nevertheless I live. And Psalm 23 became the resting place of my soul. "He restoreth my soul…" That restoration wasn't just emotional—it was strategic. He taught me how to fight with prayer and build with truth.

I remembered Walt Disney's obsession with possibility—how he saw things that didn't yet exist and pursued them anyway. That's the spirit I adopted. I didn't look for proof—I looked for purpose. I didn't wait for applause—I obeyed the whisper.

Music helped.
Movement helped.
Messiness even helped.

But what saved me was being willing to rise differently—tools in hand, strategy in heart, and oil on my life.

From Harlem to New Jersey to Vermont to Pennsylvania and back again, I never stopped collecting what I needed. Every place, every encounter added something to me. Every season required a different tool—faith, grit, forgiveness, silence, creativity, rest, courage. I honored each one.

I used to write prayers, poetry, revelations, and print them on beautiful paper and sell them. Not for the money—but as a statement of belief. That my words were part of my becoming. That my gifts were part of my war chest. That rising wasn't just something I did—it was how I healed, led, and transformed.

You can't skip processes. And you can't carry what breaks your step. A step is sacred. It's weight-tested by obedience, not decorated by what you think you can manage. I learned not to try to take shortcuts up the ladder of growth—because the rung that isn't meant for your current maturity will crack beneath you. Some weights aren't demonic—they're just not assigned to you. Let them go. Pray for clarity—not revenge. Trust that your ladder is made to carry you, not the things that tried to take you out.

Discern what enters your ear gates.

Be selective about your soul gates.

Every tool is not a weapon—some are a mirror.

Some are a lesson. Some are a light.

And for me? One of the greatest tools I will ever leave is not my résumé—it's my legacy. Not my applause—it's my inheritance. My children will inherit strategy. They will inherit strength. They will inherit an oil-soaked blueprint for how to rise—*with* God, *through* God, and *for* God. My life will speak beyond the moment. It will mark generations.

You have something to accomplish. Don't waste time. Don't dwell in dead places. Live so that your old age doesn't haunt you with the ghost of 'almost'. Feel it now so you don't waste time later.

Forgive, move, build.

Study, learn, apply.

Pray, pray again, and rise.

And when you do—do it with tools in hand.

What tools have you overlooked? What strength have you buried under survival? What blueprint is God trying to hand you if you would only open your grip from the weapons of your past?

Rise with tools, child of God. Rise with wisdom in your hand and purpose on your path. Let your healing build altars. Let your scars write blueprints. Let *your* rise leave oil for those coming next. Because you don't just survive—you construct the Kingdom.

"You don't rise once. You rise in layers. And some layers go deep before they go high."

Tools are given to those trusted with terrain. But the deeper the rise, the deeper the roots must go. She is no longer building from brokenness—she's building from depth. From soul. From knowing who she is and what she's called to do.

Tools are not just for building walls—they're for uncovering the blueprint. Every tool she picked up, was preparing her to recognize what was already placed within. Now comes the becoming. Not the invention of a new person, but the unveiling of a known one.

Before you rise into the depths, you must face what you were born into. Some chains didn't start with your mistakes — they started with your birth. This is where the rise demands more than courage; it demands confrontation.

Borndage: Breaking the Birth-Bound Chains

"You cannot rise until you face the chains you were born with, because what you inherit without consent, can still hold you without question."

"Borndage is the silent prison of the familiar. It disguises itself as normal until the Kingdom exposes it as the lie that's been holding your destiny hostage."

Your eyes are not deceiving you — you read that right. The word is borndage. It's a word I created after my own time of prayer and seeking God for how to help people identify and resolve the problems and cycles that keep showing up in their lives. Borndage is pronounced just like it looks: born-dij. It carries the weight of both birth and bondage — the chains you didn't choose but were born into. It's the limitations, mindsets, habits, and unspoken rules that you inherit without permission. And here's the dangerous part: because you were born with them, they feel normal.

Like some people, their last name, their environment, their culture, and their family's unspoken rules begin to be the very things that hold them in bondage. And the truth is, we don't get to choose those things. We don't get to choose our last names—names that, when spoken, may cause others to judge or to decide who they think we are before they even meet us. We don't get to choose the environment we are born into or the traditions we inherit. These things are chosen for us at birth.

Borndage doesn't only come through names, culture, or tradition. It can also live inside of you as illness. And here is where we must pause to understand something many never separate: emotional illness is not the same as mental illness.

Emotional illness is the breakdown of the soul's responses. It shows up in how you feel and react when life presses you. It is unhealed grief, constant anger, shame you never address, jealousy that eats away at you, or rejection that still whispers in your ear years later. Emotional illness is not always visible, but it is powerful—it shapes your patterns, your relationships, and the way you see God and yourself.

Mental illness, on the other hand, is the condition of the mind once those emotions—or other factors—begin to take root and disrupt thought, function, and balance. Mental illness can include depression, anxiety disorders, bipolar disorder, schizophrenia, or other diagnosable conditions that affect how a person thinks, feels, and behaves. It is often the fruit of many layers: biology, trauma, spiritual warfare, and yes—sometimes long-neglected emotions.

This isn't a diagnosis; it's a truth spoken from experience. I say it with reverence, knowing how fragile the heart can be when it's misunderstood. These words are not meant to replace professional care or medical help, but to bring language to what often goes unseen—to the ache that lingers long after the moment has passed.

I did not suffer from mental illness, but I did suffer from emotional illness. And that was enough to show me how dangerous it can be to ignore what you feel. Because untreated emotional illness can open the door to mental illness. One is the seed, the other the storm. One hides in silence, the other manifests in sound. Borndage is often the bridge between the two—the inherited, normalized, never-questioned cycles that make sickness feel like identity.

This is why you cannot rise until you recognize the process of both. Emotional illness must be confronted before it becomes mental illness. Borndage must be broken before freedom can be lived. Salvation makes you free, but deliverance brings you into truth. And when truth shines on the emotions you've been hiding, the mind can finally begin to heal.

Borndage doesn't always look like chains. Sometimes it looks like the familiar. It looks like tradition. It looks like culture. It looks like "the way we've always done things." But just because it's familiar doesn't mean it's right. Sometimes it's survival habits—patterns we learned in the middle of people, places, and circumstances—habits that were either forced on us or passed down so naturally that we don't even think to question them.

Borndage is dangerous because it can feel normal. When something feels normal, it's harder to stop. You don't even look for a way out, because to your understanding, this is simply life. But that's only until you have a Kingdom moment—until God Himself steps in and begins to show you what fits and what doesn't fit for your destiny.

And here is where we must address something deeper: borndage doesn't just hold you; it can corrupt and taint the way you see God. If you live too long under the weight of what you were born into, you may start to feel like God didn't know what He was doing. But He did. God, in His sovereignty, knew exactly what He was doing when He placed you in that family, in that culture, with that DNA. You were born into both strength and weakness, and the same heritage that carries your scars also carries the seed of your strength. The enemy may try to twist that placement into a lifetime of chains, but God can turn even the corrupted parts into something that serves your calling.

The difference is that you cannot allow corruption to define you. You must confront the weaknesses that come with your bloodline, your upbringing, and your learned behaviors. God allows everything, but what He allows is not always in order—so we must take His Word and use it to bring that disorder into alignment. That means facing the realities of what has been passed down and reshaping them in the light of His truth.

Some borndage isn't even about bad habits—it can look like poverty. Not just a lack of money, but a lack of belief, a lack of ethics, a lack of morals, a lack of confidence, or even a lack of understanding your own gifts. Once you begin to lack in one area, it can make you feel like there's nothing more for you.

For others, borndage is bitterness—an inherited vow that says, "We don't forgive in this family." These patterns become staples in our identity, like family rules etched in stone. "We don't marry." "We don't trust outsiders." "We don't let go." All the while, the Kingdom of God is meant to influence and transform our lives, because we have all been born for a destiny that borndage seeks to block.

Borndage can also be spiritual. There is a bondage of spiritual blindness—reciting prayers without knowing the God you're speaking to, living under religion without relationship. It is just as detrimental as any physical chain because it keeps you bound in form without freedom in spirit.

The danger in borndage is that you can spend your whole life defending it, without realizing it's destroying you. And when you finally meet Christ—the God of your salvation—when you encounter that moment that shakes you awake, you will see that the "normal" you've been protecting has been the very thing blocking your destiny.

For me, even though I was raised in church my entire life, it wasn't until I began to live the life of Christ that I realized my mind had to be retrained for the Kingdom. In order to produce in God's Kingdom, I had to release every inherited identity that didn't match who God called me to be. That release required more than willpower—it required strategic faith to see myself as God sees me, and courage to become what He spoke over me, even when I had never seen it before.

Escaping borndage means escaping dysfunctions, breaking habitual behaviors covered by spirituality, and confronting everything that tries to define you outside of Christ. And let's be honest—dysfunction shows up in all kinds of ways. Sometimes it looks like those personality types that are always chasing something new but never holding onto what's steady. It can show up in how people treat relationships, places, and opportunities like they're disposable, because they haven't found fulfillment or validation within themselves. You'll see it in the ones who always want to absorb authority over others, but never learn how to walk in equality with them. And it's there when people keep living from a false perspective of life instead of stepping into what's authentic. These aren't just quirks of personality—they're symptoms of borndage, the inherited lies that keep us searching without ever becoming. That's why the Word reminds us to "be transformed by the renewing of your mind" (Romans 12:2), because without renewal, dysfunction will always feel like identity.

It will come with silence. It will come with weeping. It will come with the experiences you've already read about in this book. But the rise begins when you identify the chains you were born with, refuse to excuse them, *and* decide to walk away from them—no matter how familiar they feel.

Salvation makes you free, but borndage must still be broken. Freedom requires a deliberate step out of what you were born into and a step into what you were reborn for. And when you do, you will finally see who you truly are and what God has always called you to be.

She rises out of her borndage.

You can't go deeper while still defending what God has called you out of. This is why your next rise will not just require strength — it will require separation. You must separate from the systems, the sayings, the cycles, and the silent rules that were never part of your Kingdom inheritance. You cannot carry borndage into the depths and expect to breathe there.

So today, I commission you:

Step out of the name that has been more curse than covering. Step out of the culture that has been more chain than compass. Step out of the survival habits that have kept you functioning but never free. Step out of the religion that gave you prayers but never presence. Step out of everything you were born into, that God never meant for you to stay in.

Rise — not with borrowed courage, but with the boldness of one who knows she is both born again and called. Rise into the depth where borndage cannot follow you. Rise into the place where destiny becomes more than a word, and freedom becomes more than a feeling. Rise into the fullness of who God saw before you were ever bound.

Emergence

"The moment you rise out of borndage, you don't just step forward — you step deeper. Freedom is not the end; it is the invitation to explore the depths of who you were always meant to be."

Breaking free from borndage is not the end of your becoming — it is the threshold. Once the chains are gone, the rise doesn't pause; it deepens. You step into the places where God refines your foundation, anchors your identity, and expands your capacity for the destiny He's always had in mind. And just like Mary, the mother of Jesus, we say, "Be it unto me according to Thy word," knowing that with that word comes everything necessary to bring us to our due season and into the full flow of God's purpose for our lives.

Depth of the Rise

"Depth demanded decisions. I made the hard ones—and Heaven saw it."

"Depth demanded my honesty. It stripped me of image and gave me inheritance."

I didn't realize how deep this would go until I was asked to choose—not just between good and bad, but between almost and aligned. It wasn't about the sins I used to run from. It was about the things I could've justified if I stayed shallow. But I couldn't stay shallow and still rise.

Depth has a way of inviting you to lower so you can rise truer. I didn't just have to let go of the wrong things. I had to let go of the right things done in the wrong season, the safe things that still stifled me, the assignments that expired and the roles that weren't mine anymore. I had to stop pretending healed just meant happy and understand that healed means whole—and wholeness means responsibility.

Be healed—because EVERYONE and EVERYTHING matters to God.
There is no such thing as great or small in the eyes of purpose.

Purpose is not ranked. Purpose is revealed. And you—you have purpose.

If you stopped measuring your life by someone else's success, would you still feel dissatisfied with your own? If the answer is yes, then there's more inside of you waiting to rise. But if the answer is no, then it's time to take what you have, who you are, and what you do—and live it to the fullest. Because you matter.

From the janitor to the CEO, from the mailroom to the boardroom. YOU matter.

Your healing begins with that truth: you matter.

No matter your title.

No matter your GPA.

No matter your platform, or your past.

You matter. And you will be strengthened and healed when you stop striving to be seen, and start living as if you already are.

I'm learning that purpose itself has depth. And with every layer came a loss. The depth of purpose often met me at the depth of abandonment. I learned to find my way through paths never laid out for me, through words never meant for my spirit, through expectations built on dysfunction. I was young—always navigating the emotions of those older than me, always making room for people who didn't even know how to sit with themselves.

So many of the storms I survived weren't mine—but I still had to find peace in them. So many emotions I had to manage weren't mine—but I still carried them, prayed through them, stood in them. I wasn't just surviving—I was rising through someone else's mess. Walking out of cycles I didn't choose, pressing through atmospheres built by rebellion, manipulation, control, and pride. That kind of terrain isn't for the weak. And the truth is: I still wanted to obey God in it.

Even when obedience made other people uncomfortable. Even when my "yes" made them question their own. Even when they didn't trust that God had a plan. And if they would've just humbled themselves to see what He was doing, we all could've risen together. But pride doesn't partner with promise. And control never walks in covenant. I never wanted control—I just wanted obedience. Even when I couldn't see past the next step. Even when His instructions didn't make sense to them—or to me.

And now, I see it. I see how He was forming me all along. I see how He used rejection to preserve me, and grief to grow me, and distance to define me. And I see how the enemy keeps some people in cycles so long they forget what change feels like. They repeat the same behaviors, the same language, the same fear—and call it discernment. But I've learned to rise from that too.

Because I am not, and you are not, the consequence of their rebellion. You are not the victim of their control, their manipulation, their deflections, their counterfeit wisdom wrapped in false spirituality. You are the result of God's tenderness and truth, of His chiseling, His healing, His unwavering vision for your life.

If they would only let Him chisel them too…if they would allow Him to father them, not just favor them…if they would surrender enough to stop building relationships from control, and start yielding to His design…they'd see it. They'd see the rise. They'd see that we are not the enemy. The enemy is the one who's kept them offended, rehearsing, stuck.

But even still—I rise. Not in arrogance, but in awareness. Because this rise came with hard choices, sleepless nights, and layers of surrender. And I wouldn't trade it. I've lived to prove my yes. I've wept through decisions that still kept me in peace. And I'm grateful for the depth of my rise.

Because when He fills the voids—when He anoints the parts that never got to live—when He breathes on the silence and births a sound out of my process…I become what the Kingdom needs. And that version of me? She is ready.

You may not have been taught how to fight from peace. You may have only known how to fight from pain, from survival, from defense. But the depth of your rise is learning the opposite—learning how to fight for peace, from peace. That means shifting your posture before you ever shift your position. It means answering chaos with stillness. And it means letting your inner calm become your greatest confrontation.

You don't have to scream to win. You don't have to hustle to prove you deserve the room. The healed you doesn't need applause to be valid. The rising you isn't looking for validation—it's looking for victory, and victory often travels through the quiet, yielding, surrendered road that most people miss.

Your perspective must now be wrapped in wisdom, not just emotion. You must see beyond the moment and respond as one who has already seen the outcome. That's what depth teaches you: not just to endure, but to govern yourself differently. This is how you break cycles without breaking down.

"I didn't rise to impress the loud—I rose to outlast the storm. My strength is quiet, but it shakes systems."

I didn't just rise—I went deep. Through abandonment, through obedience, through loss, through formation. And because of that, I carry something no shallow soul can mimic: oil that drips from depth. I am proof that the deeper the surrender, the higher the rise. And I will not apologize for how much it cost.

Now go—rise rooted, surrendered, discerning. Whether man or woman, daughter or son, this is your call to a rise that's not shallow or showy, but solid. One that doesn't just get attention—it gets results. Because when Heaven can trust you to fight like this, you become the kind of vessel God uses to reform generations.

"Truth doesn't just expose the lie—it exposes the tolerance of it. And when you stop tolerating what God never authored, that's when the real rise begins."

And just when the roots found their depth—truth called. Not the kind you recite, but the kind you live. The kind you choose even when it costs. And this next rise? It won't be soft. It will be honest. It will be holy.

Hard Choices and Holy Returns—

She Rise: Truth

"There are some truths you don't find until you bleed for them. But when you find them—you never go back."

Truth is not always a light—it is sometimes a sword. It doesn't just show the way forward; it reveals what must be left behind. And while many want to rise, few are willing to do so honestly. Because truth—real, soul-cutting, flesh-correcting, Spirit-led truth—requires a cost. It asks for decisions that don't just affect your now, but your name, your lineage, your legacy.

This kind of rise cannot be borrowed. It cannot be manufactured. It must be lived.

Hard choices will always follow holy convictions. They won't always make sense to people. They may cause others to question your obedience, your timing, even your love. But God knows. And when you choose truth in secret, God honors you in the open. That's the kind of rise this is.

This is the part of the becoming that's quiet but heavy. Not performance—but posture. Not image—but integrity. This is where altars are built in places where others built platforms.

This is the rise of return. And every return—if it's holy—starts with a decision.

We make them—and we live from them.

Choices.

Sometimes they come easy. Other times, they feel like internal surgery.

But if you're going to rise, you will have to make hard choices.

There are moments in life where obedience will ask you to do something that looks small in the eyes of others but is weighty in the realm of the Spirit. I had a vacation set aside. Everything was in place. But I didn't take my vacation in the traditional sense. I made a decision not to do something in order to do something greater. That was my offering.

And I believe God will reward me for that vacation—not just later, but in ways I didn't see coming. Because He saw the sacrifice. He saw the heart behind it.

Some of us think saying "no" means we're missing out. But real power is knowing how to say no—not just to sin, but to self. Not just to the obvious wrong, but even to good things that aren't God-things in this season. That's the discipline of alignment. That's the maturity of obedience.

We think our decisions are about preference. But when you're rising in God, your choices must be about purpose.

We don't make hard choices to look deep.

We don't do it to impress anyone.

We do it to remain faithful to the assignment.

Most of us avoid those choices because we're trying to make up for what we feel we missed. We tell ourselves we're owed something because of what we've lost. But that mindset is a trap. That way of thinking will have you chasing restoration outside of God instead of receiving holy returns through Him.

So we start bending.

We flex around obedience.

We try to stretch grace to fit our unwillingness to sacrifice.

But let me tell you—when you avoid the cost, you forfeit the encounter.

And when you forfeit the encounter, you limit the breakthrough.

That's why some of us feel stuck.

It's not that we're not called.

It's not that we're not anointed.

It's that we keep dodging the sacrifice that leads to the next door.

We end up living beneath what's possible because we won't embrace the pain of letting go.

But here's the truth:

You can make the hard choice.

You can lay it down.

You can walk away from what comforts you in the flesh to preserve what's holy in your spirit.

I'm not speaking from theory.

This isn't poetic fluff.

This is the story of my life.

I've made hard choices.

I've delayed comfort.

I've canceled plans.

I've said no to good things in order to say yes to God.

And I've watched Him respond—not just with relief, but with resurrection.

Not just with comfort, but with covenant-level evidence that He honors those who honor Him.

So yes—make the hard choice.

Let God reward what you laid down.

Let Him show you what holy returns look like.

Let Him reveal what resurrection really is—because you were willing to die to what was convenient.

This is where provision meets decision.

This is where faith becomes fire.

This is where the risen vessel becomes unstoppable.

—She Rise

May you walk forward with a faith that chooses obedience over comfort, trusting that what you lay down today becomes the divine return of tomorrow. Let the choices you make now create the covenant you carry next. Rise—and don't look back.

"Silence trained her ear. Truth trained her sound."

Once truth is told inwardly, it can't be denied outwardly. The rise begins to echo. Not in sound alone, but in essence. Her voice is no longer lost in the pain or buried in the past. It is anointed, alive, and appointed. And now—she speaks.

She Rise with Voice

"I used to whisper because I feared the echo. Now I speak because I've become it."

When healing whispers, let it echo.

There comes a moment in the rise where you realize—it's not about volume. It's not about proving anything. It's about voice. Not the one people recognize, but the one you nearly buried. The one that got silenced by pressure, muted by trauma, or sacrificed for survival. The voice that trembled in rooms where you should have been safe, and cracked under the weight of what you couldn't say.

This isn't a performance. This is presence.

This isn't an explanation. This is emergence.

Voice doesn't always come in thunder. Sometimes it's a whisper that returns in waves—subtle, sacred, steady. It's the echo of your resilience, the hum of your healing. It's the sound of trust rebuilding itself in silence. It's the moment you realized that healing doesn't always arrive with applause. Sometimes it comes with breath. Sometimes it walks in with tears. Sometimes it returns in the way you finally tell the truth to yourself.

After rising with tools, rising with truth, and rising with obedience—now I rise with voice. Not the voice of defense. The voice of deliverance.

You don't have to explain everything. You don't have to detail the betrayals or name the ones who misused your silence. You don't even have to prove you've grown. Just speak. Just live. Let your fruit speak. Let your life rise.

There is power in quiet confidence. There is healing in sacred sound. There is glory in the way your voice returns—not because the world gave it back, but because you remembered it was yours.

I remember when I couldn't speak my pain—but I could hum. And in that hum, heaven heard me. My healing began in sound, not sentence. Worship became the bridge that led my voice back home.

The voice that says, "I made it through that."

The voice that whispers, "I'm not what they said."

The voice that declares, "I still have purpose. I still have oil. I still carry sound."

A quiet room. A steady soul. Sound waves glowing with life. That's what healing can look like. Not loud—but luminous. Not forceful—but full.

Not trying to convince, just carrying truth.

To anyone who lost their sound—may you rediscover it in the wind of worship.

To every soul who hid behind "I'm fine"—may you finally speak from the deep place.

To the one who thought your silence meant defeat—may you rise with a whisper that breaks shame without ever raising your voice.

You rise with voice.

You rise with truth.

You rise with the rhythm of heaven humming inside your being.

Let your presence prophesy.

Let your decisions speak.

Let your life rise.

Because voice isn't always what you say—it's what you carry.

Jesus didn't shout at the storm. He simply said, "Peace, be still." And the wind obeyed. That's the kind of voice I rise with now.

May you walk forward with a voice that doesn't compete—but completes. May your sound be soaked in healing, your silence be strategic, and your words be wombs that birth deliverance. Speak only what builds. Declare only what heaven has written. And remember: you don't need a platform to echo—just a life that reverberates truth. Rise with voice, and let heaven hear you.

Now rise with voice that cannot be silenced. Speak when heaven prompts you, sing when your spirit overflows, and declare truth even when fear tempts you to whisper. You are not voiceless—you are victorious. You are not muted—you are anointed. Carry the sound of deliverance into every space you enter. Let your presence be prophecy, let your words be weight, and let your life be the echo of heaven.

This is your charge: Rise with voice. Speak with authority. Live with clarity. And let the world know—your sound has returned.

"Now she speaks—but not from emotion. She speaks from encounter."

But even as she speaks, she must still steward. Even as she feels, she must not be consumed. The rise of voice must be guarded by the fire of discipline. Because emotions are not altars, and tears don't always mean truth. This next rise—burn.

She Rise Word of Fire:
Your Emotions Are Not Your Altar

"The fire didn't destroy me—it discerned me. I don't worship feelings—I burn for truth."

We weren't promised ease—we were promised presence. We weren't promised convenience—we were promised strength to endure. Endurance isn't the absence of pain; it is the proof that God is with you in it. It's not easy. It's tiring. It strips us of comfort and exposes how much of our trust is in Him, not in ourselves. But how much stronger would we be if we walked like we understood the battle—even if we didn't like it?

The question is not whether the fight will come. The question is—how will you prepare? What will you do to set yourself up to stand when the fire comes to test what you've laid down? That is the greatest problem. We don't want to be inconvenienced. But who are we not to be? This life is not our own.

We lift our hands and sing the songs—
I give myself away...

But do you? Do you give yourself away when it costs you comfort? Do you still give yourself away when obedience feels like loss? It's a beautiful song. It moves emotions. But what happens when the song ends? What happens when it's no longer a melody—but a mandate? It can't just be a song. It can't be.

And I get it—most people dislike when I speak like this. But I'm not here for applause. I'm here for alignment. Applause soothes emotions. Alignment secures eternity.

Do you really want to live as an emotional wreck? Do you want people to keep speaking to your emotions only to leave you more broken? Some people know how to move you emotionally—but it fractures you mentally. You feel inspired for a moment, but your mind is left spinning. You stayed in your feelings and never accessed your future. This is where many of us miss it. It's challenging, but we need to walk in the Spirit.

We often assume that the lust of the flesh is only something sexual or sensual. But lust of the flesh is broader than that. It is anything in us that resists the Spirit of God, anything that pulls us away from His voice. It can be our appetite for comfort, our constant need to be entertained, our unwillingness to wait on God's timing, or even our search for words that soothe us but never stretch us. These are the little foxes that spoil the vine, creeping in so quietly that we often do not notice until they have already stolen from us.

The Bible tells us, "This I say then, Walk in the Spirit, and ye shall not fulfill the lust of the flesh" (Galatians 5:16). Yet what happens when we are in the Spirit, but our desire is still for God to make us feel good instead of holy? What happens when we want His presence but not His pruning, His blessing but not His breaking? What happens when we worship with words but refuse to surrender our will?

The truth is, when our emotions lead us to settle outside of the will of God, our feelings become idols. They dictate what only the Spirit should govern. And idols, no matter how disguised, will always weaken our walk. Without God, we give ourselves away to whatever soothes the moment. But with God, we give ourselves away to Him so that Christ may be formed in us. This is the true exchange of worship.

Worship is not about emotional gratification. It is not about God bowing to the rhythm of our feelings. It is about our emotions bowing to Him. True worship is when we willingly surrender our mind, our emotions, and our desires to be aligned with His Word. It is when we present ourselves as a living sacrifice, holy and acceptable to Him, which is our reasonable service (Romans 12:1).

And here is the hope: even if you have fallen short, you can rise again. Keep pressing. Fall down, get up, and press again. Release the fragmented theories that leave you spinning, and return to the simplicity of worship that aligns you with God's heart. Shut out the noise that distracts you, silence the voices that feed your flesh, and focus your worship until it becomes more than a song—it becomes your life. Worship until your heart, your mind, and your emotions are no longer scattered, but fully aligned with His glory.

Worship is not defined by the beauty of our language or the cadence of our song. Worship is defined by surrender. It is giving God the fullness of who we are, so He may reveal the fullness of who He is. And in that exchange, lust loses its power, emotions are placed in order, and we step into alignment with the glory of God.

Emotional ministry is not always spiritual ministry. And if you're not careful, you'll become addicted to feeling better without ever getting better. That's not what I came for. I'm not here to preach to your emotions. I'm here to preach to your spirit. Because the flesh has an assignment—to destroy you. But your spirit carries the authority to rise. And I came to cancel the assignment of the flesh.

That's what I had to learn. That's how I rise. I rise above situations and circumstances—not by emotion, but by Spirit. And now I'm trying to teach you how to do the same. Command your soul to respond to truth—not your emotions. Tell your emotions to bow to the hand of God. Train your soul to see beyond the moment and recognize His will. Because when you do… that's when you'll see His hand.

When you stop needing a goosebump to obey…
When you stop needing affirmation to follow…
When you stop asking for proof to believe…

That's when the will of God becomes movement in your life. Because when you no longer let your emotional state dictate your spiritual posture, you become dangerous to hell—and available to Heaven.

That's proper subduing. That's spiritual authority. That's real dominion.

He that ruleth his spirit is better than he that taketh a city.

You can't calculate God. You can't time Him. You can't box Him into your ideal timeline. The only thing you can do is be responsive to His voice.

That's what I *try* to do—every day. Whether I like it or not. Whether it hurts or not. I rise because I've learned that obedience is not optional—it's vital. My goal is not to perform. My goal is to respond. To raise my children as unto the Lord. To handle relationships, family, and ministry as an offering to God. Because if the enemy is working overtime to dishonor God's name, then I must live in a way that brings Him glory. And that is my everyday altar.

The reason why controlling your emotions is important is because emotions aren't always factual. They're real—but they're not always rooted in truth. Many people lose relationships, miss opportunities, and misinterpret divine moments because they allow undeveloped, invalidating feelings to become judge, jury, and executioner. And when those feelings are proven wrong, what's left?

We spiral into emotional torment—not because someone harmed us, but because we couldn't say no to the one thing that caused us more pain than joy: unexamined emotion.

We don't say no to the impulse to be victimized, even when our emotional outbursts make us the villain. We don't say no to the lie that because one person hurt us, everyone is trying to hurt us. We don't recognize that sometimes—life is just life. Sometimes pain is a part of growth, not a sign of demise.

Beloved, think it not strange concerning the fiery trial which is to try you, as though some strange thing happened unto you.

But emotional pain, when left in charge, distorts perception. It causes us to feel entitled to things that are not owed. It seduces us into offense when correction is trying to bless us. It leads us to mislabel the good as threatening, and the necessary as abandonment.

Emotions become dangerous when they are not brought under the subjection of stability. They must be led by truth, grounded by moral and ethical clarity, and held accountable to Spirit-led discernment. If not, we make assumptions. We cast accusations. We make altars out of our emotional needs and call it spiritual discernment. But it's not discernment—it's damage.

There is a real altar to go to—and it's not the altar of your emotions.

Your rising will only come when you learn this: Stop living for moments that make you feel spiritual. Start living for the kind of obedience that makes you be spiritual.

And when you do... you won't just rise emotionally. You'll rise eternally.

May you rise with discernment—not dependence on emotion.

May you no longer chase feelings but follow truth.

May your altar be built on obedience, not overwhelm.

Let your spirit lead.
Let your will align.
And may your life—quietly or loudly—declare:

I am no longer ruled by how I feel, but by who He is.

Rise with spiritual clarity and never bow again to the tyranny of unchecked emotions.

Now rise from this place with your spirit in command. You are not bound to moods, swings, or storms—you are anchored in the truth of God's Word. You are commissioned to walk as one who is dangerous to hell and available to Heaven. Guard your altar well. Refuse to let your emotions sit where only sacrifice belongs. Walk in dominion. Live in clarity. Carry His presence with steadfast authority. And let your life declare to every atmosphere you enter:

I rise not by emotion, but by Spirit.
I rise not for applause, but for alignment.
I rise with fire that discerns and a truth that cannot be shaken.
This is your charge. Walk in it. Rise in it. Live it.

"What she saw could never be as loud as what she knew. So she followed—eyes closed, spirit open."

After the fire, comes the surrender. The ashes become instructions. The heat reveals the hidden things. And now, she no longer needs to see the full map—she just needs to obey. She's rising not by sight, but by Spirit. Not by proof, but by promise.

The Rise of Obedience:
Seeing Without Sight

"I stopped needing proof. Obedience became my vision, and trust became my strength."

Obedience will take you through the rough and the rugged. You hear me? It will not always look pretty. It won't always come with immediate understanding or applause. But it will always come with God's hand. And that hand will steady you, correct you, lead you, and raise you—if you stay surrendered.

The problem with many of us is that we only want to obey when it's smooth—when there's a guarantee, when the road is paved, when the crowd is clapping. But true obedience doesn't wait for confirmation—it moves at the sound of His voice. It doesn't ask for details—it trusts in the direction.

I've had to walk through unfamiliar places simply because God said, *"Go."*

Not because I had the money.

Not because I had a plan.

Not because I felt strong.

But because I had a Word.

That's what obedience is. It's walking when you feel weak. It's listening when you feel lost. It's saying yes when everything in you wants to stay safe. And let me be honest with you, obedience isn't soft. It's a sharp surrender. It cuts through pride, through timing, through personal preference. It asks you to lay down your logic. It calls you to walk blindly but trust fully. It's the greatest stretch of your faith and your will.

Obedience took me through places I didn't ask for. I've been wounded in my yes. I've been overlooked, undersupported, talked about, misunderstood all while obeying. But I had to learn that following God isn't about avoiding hardship. It's about enduring with holiness. I kept walking through what I didn't understand, because I trusted the One who understood me.

That's the secret.
That's the oil.
That's the rise.

You will not see the full picture at first. But if you keep walking, you'll find that obedience creates its own clarity. God doesn't always explain—but He always establishes. And what He establishes, no man can uproot.

There were moments I wanted to quit. Moments I wanted to go back to what was comfortable. But comfort is a liar when it contradicts the call. So I kept rising. Not because it felt good—but because I refused to be disobedient.

And here's what I know now:
Obedience doesn't just change direction—it changes DNA.
It rewrites your story.
It breaks generational dysfunction.
It unlocks legacy.

My obedience will bless my children, even in areas they don't know I fought for. My yes is building altars they'll stand on.

Let me tell you again plainly: Obedience will take you through the rough and the rugged. This kind of rising doesn't float—it climbs. It scrapes against resistance. It walks over gravel, through thorns, across unseen turns. But the whole point is this—you're going somewhere. You're being led to a landing place.

So stay with the voice. Stay with the whisper. Stay with the Word. The power is not in how fast you move, but in how consistent you listen. Obedience doesn't always look like success—but it always births it.

Declare with me:

I will not let the rough places distract me from the righteous path.

I follow the voice, not the view.

I walk in obedience.

I rise through surrender.

I build in silence.

I wait in wisdom.

And even when I can't see the way—I trust that my obedience is making one.

If everything you do is about sight, you're going to miss the hand of God on your life. You won't know how to navigate the patterns He's designed for you—because everything you do is a part of the process. And when we respect the process, we honor how God is leading and guiding us.

The only way you're going to rise is if you pay attention: nothing you do is based on you. It's all about where God is trying to take you.

When you realize the uniqueness of your call...
When you understand the authenticity of your journey...
When you see how God has tailor-made your path...

You'll respond differently. You'll walk in obedience, healing, endurance, and power. And you'll begin to see the will of the Lord unfold right before you.

But until you realize this, you'll keep stumbling. You'll keep experiencing divine interruptions that you call "hiccups." Because God is trying to work something out of you—

The things that damaged you.
The things that tried to destroy your mind.
The things that belittled your worth.

And only when you silence yourself will you see the hand of the Lord. Many will never rise—because they're still too loud.

But I decree and declare in this moment:
You will learn.
You will receive wisdom.
You will receive counsel.
You will accept correction.
You will honor His "no" just as much as His "yes."
You will silence yourself and go through the process saying,
"Yes, Lord."

Not the kind of yes that picks it up and puts it down.

Not the kind of yes that obeys when it feels good and rebels when it doesn't.

But the kind of yes that is whole.

That was my journey. Even when I wrestled, I returned quickly. I didn't stay stuck in my feelings or trapped in my reasoning. Some of you stay there too long—and then expect the hand of God to move. But the hand of God cannot move until you move your opinion out of the way.

You've got to remember: His thoughts toward you are good—even when the situation isn't. Even in that, God will be glorified. Even in that, God will get you where He destined you to go.

But you must surrender. Look at the bruises. Look at the beating His Son endured. Now ask yourself: Who do you think you are to believe you'll rise without sacrifice?

But today, I choose humility.

I choose stillness.

I choose to listen.

I choose to be led.

I will not make one decision without You, God.

I will not try to navigate this life in my own wisdom.

I will sit.

I will wait.

I will obey.

I will try things Your way.

Rise in obedience, even when you cannot see. Let your yes be stronger than your logic, your surrender louder than your fear. Walk blindly if you must—but trust fully as you go. You are not led by sight—you are carried by Spirit. And when you rise in obedience, your steps are ordered, your path is secured, and your legacy is written in heaven's ink.

This is your charge:

Obey quickly.

Trust deeply.

Follow fully.

Rise with obedience, and let your life prove that faith without sight still finds its way.

"Obedience was the altar. Honor was the oil. And rising became the only option."

Obedience did what strategy couldn't. It broke the cycle. It moved heaven. It activated promise. And now—there's a lift. A final one. Not because she was perfect, but because she was willing. Not because she understood it all, but because she didn't quit.

> *"This is your rise now. You've read her story, but Heaven is writing yours."*

And even after all of this—if you still find yourself unsure, unready, undone... this next part is for you. Not for the one who feels strong, but for the one who's still shaking. Still rising anyway.

> *"I didn't rise because I was ready—I rose because I refused to stay buried."*

What Rising Looks Like on Empty

"Some risings are not born of strength, but of surrender. They are the quiet ascents of those who have nothing left to give, yet refuse to stay down."

There is a kind of rising that looks glorious from the outside, but only you and God know how much it costs. It is the kind of rising that happens when your mind is tired, your heart is worn, and you feel like you have been poured out so completely that there is nothing left for you. I know that kind of rising. It's not the poetic rise people like to post about or the dramatic comeback that gets the applause. It's the quiet, bone-deep press when you are empty and no one even realizes how much it took for you to stand up that day.

When I think about rising on empty, I think about seasons of loneliness that clung to me even in crowded rooms. I think about the quiet weight of regret—regret that whispered maybe I gave too much of myself, maybe I stayed in some places too long, maybe I tried to fix things that weren't mine to fix. But most of all, I think about the press. That relentless press not to let my situations dictate who I am or how I lead. That press to mother, to wife, to pastor, to lead, to pour, when I felt like there was no one to pour back into me at the same level.

Mental tiredness is sneaky. It doesn't always show up in obvious ways. It can feel like constant irritability, or like you're moving through life on autopilot. It can show up as forgetfulness, numbness, or that dull ache that sits in your chest and never quite lifts. People will call you strong and applaud your consistency, and they will have no idea that inside you're unraveling thread by thread. We don't talk about this enough. And because we don't, many of us keep rising on empty, believing this is just the way life has to be. It's not.

I have preached on days when I could barely hold my head up. I have held my children, my spouse, my church, my assignment together, all while feeling like I was falling apart inside. And I need you to understand, this is no disrespect to anyone who loved me or tried to be there. But I've never really had a *me* for me. Someone as solid, as consistent, as stable as I've been required to be. Someone who loved from a healed place and not from their own brokenness, someone who would go the lengths and breadths without inconsistency, without conditions. And that absence—no matter how strong you are—will drain you.

I've always tried not to overly promise and underdeliver. I've always shown up wherever I saw a need, because I never wanted to fail anybody. But when you keep doing that year after year, you find yourself living three lives in one—trying to make everybody okay, trying to hold everything together—and the cost is that you start to go empty. And the hardest part is that when you're in leadership, you don't want to bleed on the people you're assigned to. You don't want your brokenness to break someone else. So you serve. You pour. You smile. But you do it on empty.

And here's the truth we don't talk about enough: you cannot take the mental capacity of people for granted. Leaders, mothers, fathers, friends—we are not machines. People think because you're strong you'll always be strong. They think because you've been dependable, you'll always be dependable. But everyone has a capacity. And one of the reasons we end up so empty is because we've let other people's expectations pull us past that capacity without ever stopping to refill.

Awareness is the first mercy we give ourselves. Mental tiredness doesn't announce itself with flashing lights. It creeps in quietly, convincing you to just push a little harder, give a little more, say "yes" one more time. And if you're not paying attention, you'll confuse depletion for dedication. But mental tiredness isn't just a mood. It's your mind's way of saying, "I'm carrying too much". We don't always know how to name it, so we keep pressing until we collapse. But God doesn't want us to live on the brink of collapse. He wants us to see ourselves clearly, to give our souls permission to rest and recover.

It's not even that the people around you are malicious. Sometimes they don't know their own capacity either. They are frustrated by their limits, so they assume you can carry it all. They think you're judging them, when all you're trying to do is help. And when you live in that cycle long enough, it feels like the same hand you've been using to help, is the same hand being cut off finger by finger. You're left trying to function with nubs, trying to move forward, still serving, still showing up, even as you're bleeding.

There have been private battles in my life that no one will ever know. Nights when I cried out to God because I had no one who could really see me or pour into me the way I was pouring out. And in those times, the temptation is to confuse your assignment with your life. But here's what I've learned: your life and your assignment are not the same thing.

Your assignment is what God has called you to—your ministry, your purpose, your work in the Kingdom. Your life is the personal journey you are walking. And yes, they may overlap, but they are not the same. Most of our life journey is shaped by the choices we make, but our assignment is shaped by God's divine order. And if we are not careful, we start to battle publicly what's really happening privately. We start to treat every trial as if it is part of our assignment when sometimes it's just life—our choices, our relationships, our wounds.

And that's when the mental tiredness sets in. That's when you feel like you can't do anything. That's when you slip into that zombie state where you are moving but not alive, doing but not connected, serving but not rooted. And the danger of that state is that the people you're leading are only getting the best of you, not the truth of you. They're seeing the polished version, the capable version, the together version. But they don't know the cost.

There is a cost to serving on empty. There is a cost to leading while you're silently unraveling inside. But even in those moments, God taught me something I will never forget: brokenness doesn't have to cut. You can be broken and still refuse to harm the people you're called to love. You can be empty and still walk with integrity. But you also have to know when to step back, breathe, and recover your 'why'—because if your why gets lost in what you do, you'll lose yourself.

I proclaimed my resurrection three years before I saw the evidence of it. God kept emptying me and stripping me—not to destroy me, but to rebuild me. He plugged the leaks. He made me whole. He showed me that emptiness can be a holy invitation to let Him fill the spaces people cannot. And even when I felt like I had no grip left, I found I could still cling to Him because His grip on me was stronger than my grip on Him.

Rising on empty doesn't look polished. It doesn't feel triumphant. But it is holy. Because every time you rise when you could have stayed down, Heaven bears witness. And one day, the resurrection you proclaimed in faith will show up in evidence. One day you'll look back and realize: I was tired, I was drained, but I did not quit. I rose on empty—and God made me whole.

And my heart whispers this for you even now: that you would find the strength to pause, to breathe, and to let yourself be filled again. That you would know your emptiness is not failure—it is simply an invitation to receive more of what you need. May every place that has been drained, be restored with clarity and anchored again in your why. May the deep parts of you you've hidden finally heal, so that when you rise, you rise whole and not out of habit.

Even in the moments when your mind is weary and your heart feels worn, you will rise with renewed clarity and strength. You will learn to pay attention to the quiet signals of your soul, to honor your capacity, and to let God refill the places where life has drained you. You will not confuse depletion with dedication, nor will you mistake emptiness for failure.

Your private battles will not disqualify you; they will deepen you. Your assignments will not crush you; they will stretch you. Your mental tiredness will not dictate your future; it will become the place where fresh oil flows. You will rise—not just in public, but in the unseen places where no one applauds—and Heaven will bear witness.

This is your charge: rise whole, rise aware, rise free, and rise filled. Not by your own might, nor by sheer force of will, but by the Spirit of the Living God who refuses to let you stay down. Rise again, even when you're empty, and watch God make you full.

Even after I wrote these words, I sat with the reality that there will always be days when rising feels heavier than we imagined. There will always be seasons when you want to fold your hands and say, "God, I can't do this anymore." And yet—here you are. Still here. Still pressing. Still standing on the embers of what tried to burn you out.

And that is why I need to speak directly to you now. To the one who's weary but won't quit. To the one who keeps getting back up, even when no one claps for the courage it takes. To the one who is daring to rise anyway…

Wilderness – Part II: She Rise Through the Wilderness: Becoming While Waiting

"This is not a new wilderness—it's the other side of it."

The wilderness is not just a place. It is a reality—an environment of stripping, reshaping, and sacred stillness that doesn't wait for your comfort to complete its work. It wasn't the desert that scared me, it was the realization that I was not who I thought I was. It was the awareness that even though I was surrounded by people, there were parts of me that were being raised alone. By the time life started introducing grief, disappointment, unexpected shifts, and delays—I had already learned how to live in silence, how to hear beyond noise, and how to follow the invisible pull of the Holy Spirit.

I often say that I was raised in the jungle—by the Holy Ghost. Yes, there were people around. Guardians. Community. Church. But still, there were moments that felt like divine isolation. I couldn't always explain it. I wouldn't dare blame anyone. But I knew early that there was a different set of hands on me. And those hands didn't always lead me the easy way. They led me through places where things didn't grow. Through paths where vision was hard to see. Through terrain where I felt foreign, even in familiar places.

In the wilderness, you don't just realize where you are—you realize who you are not. I had to admit that I was deeply intertwined with people, not just because of love, but because I was searching for a kind of filling. I didn't yet understand that some of what I was calling 'connection' was actually a cry for covering. I wasn't just loving people—I was leaning into them as a substitute for the things I lost and never got back. The wilderness taught me that not every loss gets a replacement. Some people don't get restorations in the way they imagined. Some wounds never close the way we wanted them to. And not everything you love will stay.

But the wilderness is also where I learned not to resent that. It's where I found out that healing doesn't always mean reversal—it often means release. And that's not easy to explain when you're still bleeding from what left you. But in that desert, I came face to face with the Spirit of God in a way that changed how I walk, how I hear, and how I wait.

No one really understood how much my ears had to stay tuned to God. I don't mean that in offense. But I was so hungry for love, so desperate to belong, that I couldn't see how God was positioning me to follow His voice—more than I followed familiarity. The deeper I tried to belong to others, the more God revealed I had to belong to Him. He didn't want my dependency—He wanted my devotion. And that difference cost me a lot. Relationships didn't always last. Not from confusion, not from offense, but from design. People didn't always stay. And I couldn't always explain why, but it became clear that I wasn't being denied—I was being designed.

There's a version of me that I would've never met if the wilderness hadn't taught me. She didn't rise with applause. She didn't rise with understanding. She rose with scraped knees, tear-stained prayers, and a quiet knowing that God was up to something deep, even if it was slow.

And I've had to carry that same wilderness wisdom into every part of my life. Even when I became a wife young—even when I stepped into adulthood before I could finish healing from childhood—I was still being raised by the Holy Spirit. Every decision, every opening, every closing…it was all Him. And I didn't always like how it felt. But I knew it was God. That's the tension of the wilderness—it is painful and prophetic at the same time.

What makes the wilderness sacred, is that it breaks you down in places that sermons don't always touch. It doesn't ask for your opinion. It doesn't wait on your maturity. It just happens. And in it, you either collapse into your confusion—or you learn how to rise in the silence of delay. You learn how to survive without substitutes. You learn how to stand tall even when you feel like screaming. You don't fake strength. You just stop fearing surrender.

And that's where I met Mowgli. Or better yet—that's when I became Mowgli from Disney's, The Jungle Book. Because I understood what it meant to be in a wild world, guided by a Presence nobody else could see. I was in the jungle of life, and yet…I never wandered. Not because I was brilliant. Not because I always had clarity. But because the Spirit of the Lord led me through it. He opened doors. He shut others. He shifted my steps in moments that made no sense at all. And I had to let Him.

This chapter won't fit most. And I've learned through life that one of the ways we're destroying people is by refusing to understand variety. God moves in different ways for different people. And if this doesn't look like your life—it's okay. You may not have walked this path. You may not have encountered this terrain. But everyone will have something to encounter individually. And I'm writing for those people. I'm living for those people. I've learned in the wilderness that I don't have time to be a critic of someone else's experience. God gives each of us an audience. A specific tribe. A divine assignment. And I believe if we honored that, the world would be more peaceful. People would emerge from wilderness experiences not deluded—but focused. Because when you understand the mission of God for your life, you stop trying to mimic someone else's encounter.

There's a big world, full of diverse callings, trials, and testimonies—and we have to learn to agree with the fact that we don't always understand someone else's process. Respect the wilderness experience. Just like many didn't respect Jesus'. He had Sadducees and Pharisees who always had an opinion—even while He was fulfilling prophecy. And some of us have walked through wildernesses that reflect exactly who Jesus is—not out of formality, but out of revelation, out of a witnessed testimony, out of a real walk. You may not have made it through what I survived. You may not have been able to stand through what tried to destroy me. But don't deny my witness. Don't dismiss someone's rhema just because it doesn't resemble your reality.

And I also want to say this: just like you may not understand my walk, there are people whose journeys I have not walked either. And I celebrate their survival. I celebrate their witness. I celebrate the strength it took to endure what I may never know. I believe there's a kind of trust that God places on those of us who walk through hardship—not because we are better, but because He knows we won't turn on Him. Celebrate your journey. Celebrate your testimony. Celebrate the revelation that comes from your private walk with God. And know that if you're still holding on, it means God still trusts you to carry what you've been through without denying who He is.

I'm not claiming to be a map. But I am a memory. And I know what it feels like to survive what had no exit plan. So now I rise…not because I conquered the wilderness. I rise because the wilderness couldn't stop what God had already planted in me.

There are no easy roads to becoming. And the wilderness will never apologize for how it breaks you. But if you let it teach you, if you let it shape your appetite, refine your hearing, and discipline your reach—you will rise in ways that comfort could never have birthed. The silence is sacred. The solitude is sanctifying. And the outcome? It's not just strength. It's clarity. And that clarity will outlast every loss.

Father, I thank You for every dry place that formed me. For every closed door that centered me. For every unanswered question that pulled me back into Your voice. Let the wilderness not be wasted. Let it make us wise. Help us stop measuring life by how fast we get out—and teach us how to live well while we're still in it. Lead us by Your Spirit the way You did with Jesus. The way You did with me. And let our rise be evidence that You were with us the entire time. Amen.

I rise without needing clarity to obey.
I rise without substitutes to sustain me.
I rise without replacements for what I lost.
I rise from the wilderness—not just with survival, but with sight.

I rise because God raised me with no witnesses, and still called me worthy.

If you've ever felt misunderstood because your wilderness didn't look like someone else's victory—take heart. If you've ever felt alone while being led—don't give up. There is a tribe, a call, a rise, and a revelation that has your name on it. You are not invisible. You are being formed.

The Pharisees would have missed it. But the wilderness dwellers would recognize.

This is gospel.

Because Jesus was led into the *wilderness* by the Spirit.

Because John preached from the *wilderness* before he pointed to the Lamb.

Because Moses met God in a burning bush in the *wilderness*.

And because you—like them—have emerged not empty, but anointed.

The wilderness is not a punishment. It is not a curse. It is not the result of disobedience by default. And it is not to be pitied or prematurely escaped. The wilderness is the divine classroom where revelation is tested and encounter is initiated. It is the place where faith is not weakened—it is rooted. Where the Word is not just spoken—it is lived. It is the place where oil is not only poured—it is crushed into being.

This is my theology. Not opinion. Not comfort. Not even personal interpretation alone—but a studied and lived conviction born from the presence of God. I've learned that the wilderness is the training ground of those whom God will trust with His secrets. The hidden ones. The seekers. The intercessors. The obedient. The hungry. The yielded. The ones who don't need applause to keep walking or clarity to keep trusting.

The wilderness is the place of divine design.

This is not a motivational closing. This is a commissioning.

You don't just exit the wilderness—you are sent from it. And when you are sent, everything shifts. You speak differently. You walk differently. You discern differently. And you move with heaven behind you. You no longer chase validation. You no longer need escape. You no longer beg for understanding. You realize: the wilderness did something holy to you. And even when no one else sees it—God does.

I must confess something now: there was a long time in my life where I felt like I was trapped in a version of The Truman Show. If you've ever seen it, you know what I mean. A man unknowingly raised inside a fabricated world, always seeking 'the door', always suspicious that everything around him was orchestrated—false, repetitive, and scripted. That's what life felt like for a long time. Repetitive patterns. Cycles I couldn't explain. Pain that seemed too aligned to be random. I used to think I was Truman—searching for the exit.

But I was wrong.

I'm not Truman. I'm not just looking for a door anymore. I've learned to find purpose in something that seems never-ending. And in that surrender, something changed. I stopped counting the days, and started making the days count. I stopped looking for the finish line, and started trusting the divine pace. This is not about exiting anymore—it's about emerging with wisdom. Purpose. Depth.

And now I want to say this to you. Every part of your life matters. Every wilderness season. Every silence. Every detour. Every delay. Every moment that felt like a loop—it was doing something sacred. So stop always looking for the exit. Learn to honor the unfolding.

Because every part of your life has weight. It has value. It has voice. Even the hardest parts. They weren't just there to break you. They were there to prove your strength when you didn't even want to be strong. To reveal your creativity when you didn't feel like producing anything. To show you your endurance when you were ready to collapse. That's not a survival story. That's a witness.

You've been given the gift of life—not a theatrical performance, but a real, raw, Spirit-led, unfiltered life. And if you pour your oil into that, if you show up with truth and love and obedience—what you'll reap can't be stolen. Because the wilderness did it. God authored it. And the fruit is undeniable.

I am a witness.

I see the fruit of my labor every single day.

I see it in the breath I still carry.

I see it in the people I lead.

I see it in the strength I never asked for but still own.

And no one can take credit for it but God.

Not culture. Not a crowd. Not a committee.

God did it. The wilderness did it.

And I will never deny it.

Even with the sabotages.

Even with the betrayals.

Even with the long stretches of no clarity—

I was never supposed to end here.

That's the miracle.

That's the message.

That's the rise.

> This girl from Harlem who survived it all, didn't rise with hype—

She rose with heaven.

She rose with wilderness wisdom.

She rose with holy silence.

She rose with divine commissioning.

And now…

She Rise.

From Wilderness to Wind:
The Rise Doesn't End, It Deepens

"The wilderness gave me roots. The wind gave me wings. And together, they taught me how to rise without end."

She didn't just rise from the wilderness—she rose with it.

The dry places didn't disqualify her. They defined her. And now, as the dust settles and the silence sharpens, a new wind begins to stir—not to erase what was, but to carry it forward. This next breath isn't separate from the wilderness—it's the result of it. It's what happens when the wilderness turns into wisdom. When the waiting turns into wind. When the rise is no longer just upward, but inward.

You've walked with her through the ache. You've heard the echo of delay. You've seen the places where fire met faith. And now…you stand at the threshold of the Final Lift.

Let this be your inhale.

Let this be your cue to rise—again, and again, and again.

"The wilderness gave me more than a way out—it gave me a way forward. The proof of survival is not in the scars you carry, but in the wisdom you refuse to leave behind."

The wilderness may have emptied me, but it also anchored me. Every lesson learned here is not just survival—it is the final lift, carrying me out with more strength, more clarity, and more God than I had when I entered. Every rise leaves behind a trail of truths—lessons forged in storms, confirmed in silence, and proven in victory. Before I close this journey, I want to place them in your hands, not as theories, but as weapons, tools, and anchors for your own rise.

She Rise: Lessons Learned

"These are not just lessons—they are landmarks, proof that God met me in every valley and shaped me for every mountain."

Every rise comes with scars, questions, and truths that cannot be unlearned. This is not the chapter where I reteach what I've already said—it's the chapter where I gather it all in my hands and pass it to you as my final impartation. These are not theories. They are the kind of lessons you only learn when you keep walking after the night fell, when you kept showing up even with the limp, when you chose to be healed while still in motion. If my journey has taught me anything, it's that you don't wait until you're perfect to rise—you rise, and in rising, you keep becoming.

Even if this seems far from your reality—as it still is for me—don't deny truth just because you're still becoming it. Hold fast to the truth and let God bring you into His perfect will.

I've learned that you can't be a spiritual parent without growing from being a child yourself. And when we've come from mismanaged homes—emotionally, mentally, or spiritually—we can carry that same mismanagement into the lives of those we lead if we don't confront it. I can only speak for my life, but I know this much: even when God has called you, you must keep growing. I never wanted to be full of the Word but empty of the believer's character. There is a way for the believer to live. I choose to rise matured, not just aged.

I don't want to write a whole lot of corrective posts and never identify if that's what I do or how I handle people. So I begged the Lord—make me conscious. Never let me become a sounding brass or a tinkling cymbal. Keep me alert and aware so that my mismanaged pain never defines my rise. Heal me as You call me. Heal me as You save me. Rewire me as You deliver me. Fill me as You empty me. Prepare me as You sanctify me.

When we call borndage the borndage it really is, we won't be afraid to grow out of "that's just the way I am," or carry hidden, nasty character and cover it with a smile. True deliverance is like having good customer service—the genuine heart to serve with a smile, not with envy, anger, or a lack of true ability to want to help. That's the kind of deliverance I want to walk in, and the kind of deliverance I want to see in those who rise. Because rising without it is just dressing wounds with new titles, while the infection still spreads.

This is how we mature and move past opinion—gospel filled with theories, ideas, logic, and words—into a life that becomes a testament of who God is in His power, authority, and strength. And the only way we can get there is to walk into our healed places. Not places that destroy, but places that unite. Places where we can rightly divide the Word we stand on, and then live it out in the marketplace, in ministry, and in whatever sphere of influence we are assigned to—whether that's in the home, in government, in education, in business, in the arts, in media, or in the church. It's the process that shifts us from what life made us, to what God created us to be.

I've watched what happens when this is missing, and I refuse to be part of the problem when God has called me to be part of the solution. Your healing is important. Everyone may not rise in the same way, but be humble enough to stand before wisdom and receive it. Don't reject it. Rejection keeps your unhealed places from receiving the nourishment they need to fit into a fully grown body. Your mind must grow just like the rest of you.

Some are still chasing attention, still doing childish things wrapped in adult language, calling it discernment and authority. I asked God to save me so thoroughly that I would never walk in my own thoughts about people, places, or things—but only in *His* mind. He is the Author and Finisher, the Alpha and Omega. I cried, "Lord, let me know what that really means so I can be true to my entire calling."

It's not about being perfect. It's about continuing to mature in the places that will make you evidence of God's power, not proof of man's weakness. Yes, you'll have a thorn—something that keeps you humble. But even in that, never forget Who is in control, Who you serve, and Who hired you for this work. Rise in healing. Rise with understanding. Rise with sensitivity to the time and the space you're in, so nothing God has placed in your hand is neglected or abused because of unhealed places.

Never rise so high that you stop receiving instructions that are meant to grow you. If we are to be the image of God, we must accept that this work will continue until the day we die. Good instructions without fullness of character can hinder the very reason we exist. So rise healed—because whenever there is a dilemma in the earth, it starts where the light was supposed to shine.

I don't want to be a shadow or an artificial light. I want to be light. Not just light that glimmers in the darkness, but light that exposes, heals, and transforms. That's how you rise in the fullness of power and authority. That's how you mature into the assignment God has placed on your life. That's how you rise healed.

I have learned that rising in silence can be louder than defending yourself. Sometimes God's vindication is not in proving your point but in revealing your fruit.

I have learned that strategies birthed in prayer are stronger than reactions birthed in pain.

I have learned that humility is not weakness; it is the gate that keeps the oil flowing.

I have learned that the wilderness is not punishment—it is preparation. And those who learn to worship there will not break when the platform comes.

I have learned that the same God who gave me power, gave me boundaries, and that keeping them is as spiritual as casting out a demon.

I have learned that some doors are not locked; they are simply waiting for me to grow into the stature that fits the key.

I have learned that rising healed is not a one-time event, but a rhythm—a daily exchange of my wounds for His wholeness.

I have learned that deliverance is not only from demons, but from mindsets that keep us acting like slaves when we are already sons and daughters.

I have learned that authority without compassion will crush people, but compassion without authority will leave them bound.

I have learned that hearing what the Spirit is saying is not enough—you must also learn how to deliver it according to your role, not your gender. Kingdom assignments are not male or female; they are Spirit-led, Spirit-formed, and Spirit-empowered.

I have learned that the crowd's applause can't confirm your calling, and their silence can't cancel it.

I have learned that offense is a choice, and forgiveness is a decision you make before you feel it.

I have learned that some people are not toxic—they are just not assigned to walk with you past a certain season.

I have learned that waiting on God is not passive; it is the active trust that works while it waits.

I've learned that some "covenant" spaces are really control, disguised as unity—limiting the vastness of a big God to a single mold. That mindset has to be shattered.

I've learned that kindness can be mistaken for weakness, causing some to withhold what you are due—whether it's honor, respect, or revenue. So you must know your worth, take the lesson from every situation, and live from that truth.

I've learned—and want to teach—that every person is special in their own right, and you never have to be intimidated by someone else's nature. God created a unique one in you. There is a mold only *you* can fill, and it carries something the world needs—something the earth is requiring.

I've learned that watered-down juice loses its strength—and in the same way, when we dilute who we are by neglecting the wisdom passed down to us, we forfeit the elevation and supernatural life God intended. Just as watered-down juice can't offer its full nutrition, we cannot rise into our supernatural identity without fully becoming ourselves and embracing the wisdom handed to us.

I've learned that family is not only defined by blood. God has taught me the true meaning of family through those He ordained to walk with me—Kingdom-minded people who love without condition. To those who feel disenfranchised or without relatives, know that God will place you in a tribe that sees you, values you, and covers you.

I've learned the difference between broken pieces and shattered—because broken pieces can still fit together to make a masterpiece.

I've learned that every ounce of who I am is a piece of God's puzzle, designed to fit perfectly into the spot He has prepared for me.

I've learned that what I've come through is never an indication of what I'm not—it's a vivid picture of who I am. And when I live from that truth, drawing strength from every lesson, I become what I was ordained to be.

I've learned that I don't wake up every day with something to do; I wake up with something to be.

I've learned to respect time by not wasting it on should've, could've, or would've, but by exhausting the calm, the rush, the sacred moments—the flow of each day. Every day has a flow. Tap into it.

I've learned to pray for the unhealed and immature so that life and time are not stolen from them.

I've learned that sometimes we can't just stand in the gap—we must fill the gap.

I've learned how to not box God according to my limited sphere and to let Him grow me into the fullness of this large yet small world we live in.

I've learned to honor progress without skipping process for lack of patience.

I've learned to allow the Holy Spirit to allocate where and what I digest so I won't become spiritually fragmented.

I've learned to enlighten without offense, because we have to understand that people don't want their intelligence tested when it's still too closely tied to their self-esteem. This can cause us to become rigid and not allow God's Word or wisdom to flow through us, because we're stuck on what we think we know.

I've learned that love is what love does, but it is also defined by the limitation of your exposure and your healing.

I've learned it's better to go into the book than just read the cover—that's how I deal with people too.

I've learned that *loss* does not make you *lose* when you grieve properly.

I've learned to respect the resources of God by not limiting them to my personal preferences.

I've learned that every day and every step matter, to make sure I'm not just a fig tree that looks full but has no fruit.

I've learned to value every day and every minute—that every time my eyes catch my birth date on the clock, I command myself to live, to learn, and to reset. No matter what, I was born for purpose.

I've learned that every year of my life is too full to be a single chapter—I am a series, a sequence of evolving plots in a full story.

I've learned to exhaust every resource, so you will meet the Source at every destined point of your path.

I've learned to never place my value on the applause of man, because man may never know how to clap for the new-yet-old thing that springs forth—just like when Jesus entered the earth.

I've learned that if people can keep you small, they will love you.

I've learned to never fight immaturity with anger—fight it with intelligence.

I've learned to be more observational than judgmental, because you learn so much more of God outside the box of your reality when you pay attention beyond your fragmented sight.

I've learned to recognize when a season is over and not to stay there, because it will cause you to be out of alignment—and that misalignment can bring delays that sometimes we cannot recover from.

These are my lessons learned. They were not taught to me from the comfort of a classroom, but in the press of life, in the weight of responsibility, and in the call of God that would not let me stay the same. And if you take nothing else from my rise, take this: ask Him to heal you as He calls you, so you don't just carry the Word—you carry His nature. Because a healed leader rises differently. They rise not only for themselves, but so that nations can breathe again.

"Strength is the lesson proven—when what you've endured turns into what you now embody."

Every lesson she carried became more than survival—it became a foundation. And foundations, when tested, reveal not just what you know but who you have become. Lessons turn into strength when they are lived, and strength becomes the evidence that nothing has been wasted.

She Rise with Strength

"True strength is not in how much you can carry, but in how much you can surrender—and still rise."

Strength has always been misunderstood. People think it's about muscles, about appearing invincible, about never bending under pressure. But strength in the Kingdom is paradoxical. It's layered, costly, and often pressed out of pain. It's the quiet endurance of one who keeps rising even while still bleeding. It's the love that forgives when betrayal cuts deep. It's the worship that doesn't stop even when walls have fallen. My strength has not been loud or shallow—it has been resilient and redemptive.

I have learned that you can be personal without exposing all of yourself. That's part of my strength. The world pressures you to overshare, to tell it all, while others guard their secrets and still use your tools. But true strength learns stewardship of story. I can give you the tools that built me without handing you every wound. And some of you reading this need to learn the same: you can be personal and yet remain private. It doesn't make you less authentic; it makes you wise.

What people didn't understand about me was this: how could I keep loving without turning on the ones who betrayed me? How could I forgive when the offense cut so deep? How could I choose to glorify God in situations where it would have been easier to satisfy my flesh? They called it weakness, but the paradox of the Kingdom says otherwise. When you are weak, then you are strong (2 Corinthians 12:10). That's not just scripture to me—it's survival. It's the paradox that has kept me from becoming bitter, from letting betrayal define me, from letting pain dictate my choices.

Strength is also about sincerity. I never claimed to be perfect. But I do strive to be sincere—with God, with people, with myself. And in a world that values masks and appearances, sincerity itself is strength. I've learned that perfection is a trap, but sincerity is a testimony.

My life has carried traumas that could have killed me. Losing my mother, my city, and the family I knew—all in what felt like a single breath—was more than anyone should have to bear. And people don't guide you through trauma; they judge it. They tell you how you should feel, how long you should grieve, what steps you should take to recover. But strength is not in pretending trauma didn't happen. Strength is in refusing to let trauma replace your testimony. I learned how to love people through their own pain because I understood the bigger picture, not from a narrow, shallow view.

I see my strength in unexpected places in scripture. Ezekiel saw dry bones and devastation, but his strength was in vision—seeing life where others only saw death. Nehemiah faced broken walls and scattered people, but his strength was in rebuilding with accountability and prayer. Moses did not try to play God; he went up to seek God, and then came back down with His word. Job, afflicted beyond measure, could have decided that God didn't love him—but instead, his endurance showed us that faith can survive suffering. And David—David refused to let anything stop his worship, even in imperfection. These men of God weren't perfect, but they carried strength that was sincere, paradoxical, and rooted in their relationship with the Lord.

That's how I see myself. Not flawless, not always understood, but unwilling to let anything stop my worship, unwilling to let anything steal my testimony, unwilling to let anything distort my love for God. I am not striving to be impressive; I am striving to be faithful. That's strength.

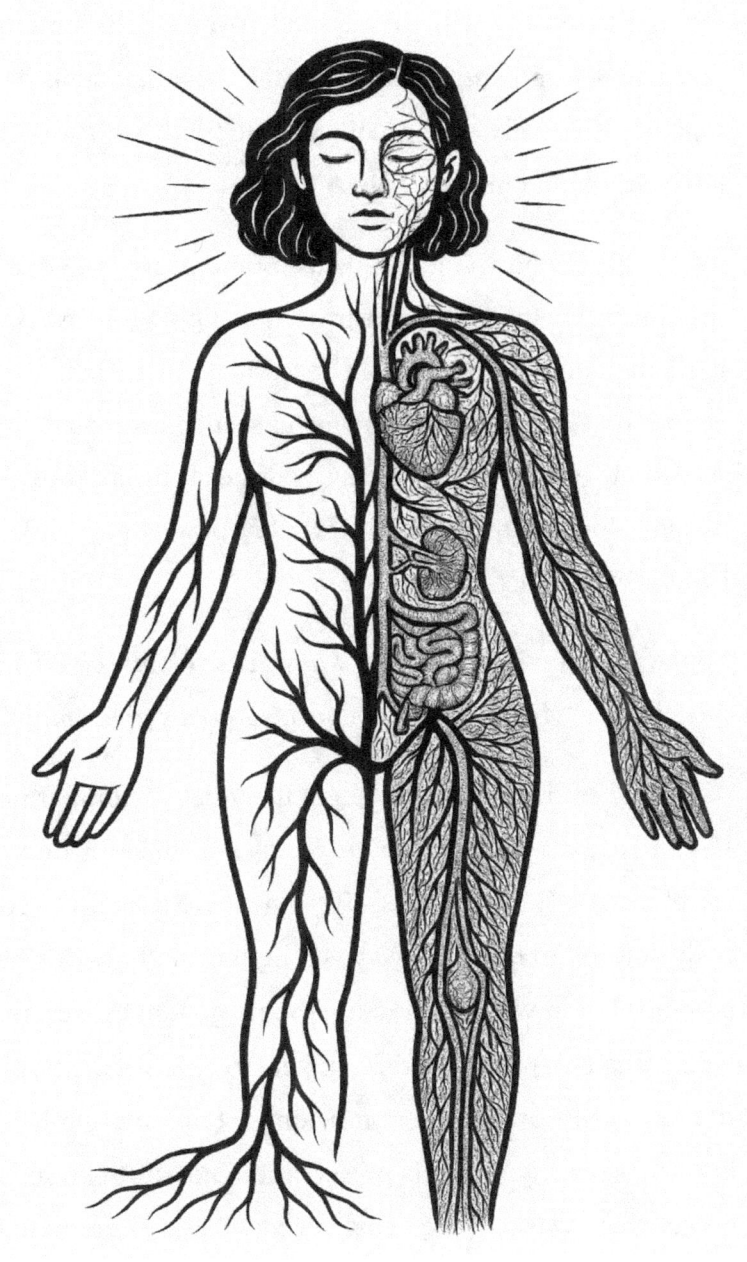

Imagine the human body. Muscles may look like the strongest part, but without the hidden veins carrying blood, the unseen bones holding structure, or the quiet ligaments binding it together, the body would collapse. Strength isn't found in one part—it's found in the whole.

That's how God builds us. Some people in your life are the fingers, helping you grasp what's slipping away. Some are the shoulders, steady enough to carry your weight when you can't. Some are the veins, flowing unseen, but keeping you alive. And some are the neck, turning your head toward direction and vision. None of them are the whole body—but together, they become strength.

So the question is never, *"Do I have enough muscle?"* The question is, *"Am I valuing the parts God has given me?"*

There is a kind of strength that doesn't come from holding on, but from letting go. Veins are made for flow, not for blockage. If blood is cut off from where it needs to go, the body suffers. In the same way, strength is not only in what you embrace but in what you release. Some goodbyes feel like a vein being cut, painful and final, yet God allows them so that life can keep flowing where it belongs. True strength is knowing when goodbye is preservation, not destruction. You do not grow weaker when God severs what was draining you—you grow stronger because His flow is redirected into purpose.

"Strength is not the muscle you show—it's the life that flows unseen through every vein God designed."

Think about the veins in the human body. I've learned, if you could lay them end to end, they would stretch for more than sixty thousand miles—enough to circle the earth more than twice. And yet we rarely notice them. They run beneath the surface, hidden, carrying life every second of every day.

That's how God works with strength. What looks hidden, what feels overlooked, is often carrying the most weight. You can't see forgiveness flowing, but it's keeping you alive. You can't always see worship in a storm, but it's fueling your spirit. You can't measure grace by surface appearance, but like veins, it stretches farther than you can imagine.

So when I rise with strength, it's not just because I've flexed a muscle—it's because I've trusted the unseen flow of God's design. What people call small, God calls sustaining. What people overlook, God multiplies.

Strength is not only measured in how much you can resist—it is also measured in rhythm. Just as the veins carry a steady pulse, strength is often found in quiet consistency, not in loud defiance. Anyone can rise once with adrenaline. But true strength is getting back up every day with the same steady pulse, the same determination, the same yes to God. Rhythm sustains what resistance alone cannot. My survival has not only been about dramatic moments of triumph, but about daily choices to keep the beat of faith when everything around me was trying to break my cadence.

I have also discovered that strength is not built in isolation—it is built through the body. Too often we look for one person to be everything for us, when God assigns different parts to different people. Some are the fingers, some the shoulders, some the veins, some the neck. Each one matters. Each one supplies something you need. We think strength is about finding the muscle, but God reminds us it's also about veins, bones, ligaments, vessels—all working together. Strength is in valuing every part God sends into your life, not elevating false covenants or sarcastic companions, but discerning who truly carries a role in your rise.

Veins remind us of exchange. They do not simply carry blood; they carry life through a constant give and take—oxygen exchanged for carbon dioxide, nourishment exchanged for waste. Strength is not just what you give out, it is also what you allow in. Too many of us collapse because we exhale constantly but never inhale. We pour out love, counsel, forgiveness, service, but do not allow God to breathe back into us. My strength has not only been in what I release, but in what I receive from Him. Without intake, strength dies. But when you allow the hidden exchange of Spirit to refill you, you find you can keep rising without collapsing.

That is why I've learned to look at people through Kingdom eyes. Not based on their status, not based on temporary revelations, but based on the heart and the part they play in God's design for my life. And just like the body of Christ, every joint supplies (Ephesians 4:16). Somebody may be the finger in your life, somebody else a shoulder, somebody the neck. If you miss their value because they don't look like a muscle, you miss the strength God has given you.

So yes, I rise with strength. Not because my life has been without weakness, but because weakness has been the very place where His power is made perfect. That's the paradox of the Kingdom. When you grasp that paradox, you discover that strength is not about what you can hold up—it's about what God holds together in you.

I rise with strength because I've learned that…

When I lose, I actually gain.
When I am weak, then am I strong.
When I forgive, I am freed.
When I let go, I am lifted.
When I release my rights, I discover His righteousness.

When I stop fighting to be seen, Heaven makes me known.

When I embrace my wounds, I also uncover my wisdom.

When I worship in imperfection, I encounter perfect love.

When I die to myself, I live unto Him.

These are not contradictions; they are confirmations of Kingdom truth. And once you understand them, you know you are walking in strength. Strength is not about proving anything to people. Strength is about proving God faithful through your life.

That's why I can say without hesitation: She Rise with Strength.

Strength is never meant to stop at survival. God did not weave sixty thousand miles of veins into the human body just to keep us barely alive. He designed them to reach every part, to expand into places unseen. In the same way, my strength is not just that I endured wounds or survived trauma—it is that I expanded. I stretched into new dimensions of calling, writing, leading, and building. Survival is strength at its beginning. Expansion is strength at its fulfillment. She rises with strength not just to hold herself together, but to multiply into new territories where God has destined her to flow.

Lord, I thank You that true strength does not come from flesh but from Spirit. Teach us to value every part You assign to our lives—the veins, the bones, the ligaments, the hidden members that make us whole. Give us discernment to know who belongs to our body, and courage to release who does not. Teach us to forgive when it seems impossible, to love when betrayal cuts deep, to worship when the walls around us fall. Let our strength be sincere, not performative. Let our strength be paradoxical, rising in weakness and perfected in grace.

I declare: I rise with strength. My weakness is not my end; it is the stage where God's power is made perfect. My trauma is not my cage; it is the soil where testimony grows. My life is not my own; it is the vessel where God's glory will be revealed.

Now, rise in the strength of God. Not in the shallow kind that people measure, but in the paradoxical power that only Heaven understands. Rise with the strength that forgives when it hurts, worships when it's weary, and loves when it would be easier to walk away. Rise with the strength that values every part God has placed in your life and refuses to despise the hidden joints and unseen veins. Rise with the strength that proves God faithful through your testimony. Now—she rise with strength.

"Strength steadies you; consciousness awakens you. Together they shape your rise."

Strength steadies the frame, but sight directs the frame. What good is lifting if you do not know where to carry? What good is standing if you cannot see what you're standing for? Strength brings you through battles, but consciousness teaches you why the battle mattered. Strength is the foundation, but consciousness is the revelation.

"Strength built the foundation, but consciousness opens the eyes to see where to build next."

She Rise in Consciousness

"Strength without sight stumbles, but consciousness gives power its purpose."

Strength without consciousness is blind. You may have muscles, motion, and even momentum, but without awareness, you're swinging in the dark. To rise in consciousness is to rise in strength that sees. Being aware is not just survival—it is wisdom. You must be aware of the enemies who come against you, but just as importantly, you must be aware of the inner me who can sabotage you. You must be aware of your needs as well as your wants. Aware of the world around you and not just your own private universe. Consciousness sharpens you, opens you, and steadies you.

Consciousness perfects your mathematic skills, because our God is always working in the deep equations of life. He multiplies peace when chaos should have consumed you. He multiplies grace where sin abounded. He multiplies strength in weakness until you realize His power was the answer all along. He adds years to a life the enemy tried to shorten. He adds wisdom where you once only had wounds. He adds people into your journey who carry you further than you could have walked alone. Yet addition is not always easy—it often comes with responsibility, with the weight of stewardship. He divides burdens so you don't carry them alone. He divides you from relationships, systems, and environments that would choke your destiny. Division is painful, but consciousness reveals it as deliverance. And He subtracts chains so you can walk free. He subtracts idols so you can see Him clearly. Subtraction may feel like loss, but in God's math it is always protection. This is not surface arithmetic—this is the divine calculation of a God who hardened Pharaoh's heart, who moved kings like pieces on a board, who multiplied loaves from lack, who subtracted Egypt's hold from Israel with a single night of deliverance. Consciousness teaches you that every equation is intentional, every calculation is precise, and every number He works out is meant to bring you into alignment with His will.

 Consciousness will cause you to enjoy your God and your world from a childlike view—not causing you to be childish, but teaching you to wonder again. That difference is vital. Childishness is immaturity; childlikeness is worship. Childishness complains in the wilderness, but childlikeness marvels at manna. Childishness throws tantrums when it doesn't get its way, but childlikeness throws praise even when it doesn't understand the way. Childishness wants the blessing without the process, but childlikeness trusts the Father through every process. One breaks under weight, the other turns weight into worship. Consciousness keeps you childlike—open, trusting, full of awe—while killing what is childish—fragile, selfish, unstable. It is the difference between refusing to grow and choosing to remain teachable. Consciousness makes you lean into wonder without losing your wisdom.

Consciousness makes you sensitive to the world you speak, because you understand the world you shape. You stop living off slogans and start shaping atmospheres. You begin to discover what you really feel and believe about your God, not just what you say to people to sound strong, smart, or settled. You are not afraid to express your thoughts and feelings to God—even when they sound raw, even when they sound wrong—because you no longer need Him to agree with you. You just need Him to be God, and you need to be real before Him.

Consciousness makes you accept a God decision. You don't wrestle against it, you work with it. That is the moment where you ask Him, "Teach me how to apply Your math skills to my situation." Life is shorter than long, and most of us have more years behind us than before us. No matter your age, stage, or circumstance—you are still allowed to wake up. Life isn't scary, it's a labyrinth full of ins, outs, twists, and turns. But you—yes, YOU—have already been given tools, voice, strategy, and wisdom if you asked for it. Consciousness is the key that shows you where to use them.

Consciousness also teaches you this truth: the war is already won. Yet God, in His sovereignty, leaves you the residue of the battle. Why? Because power is useless if you never have to use it. He gave you power for a reason. Residue doesn't mean defeat—it is evidence of victory. David still had to pick up a stone and swing it, though God had already delivered Goliath into his hand. Israel still had to march around Jericho, though the walls were already scheduled to fall. Jesus still left us with demons to cast out and storms to calm, though the cross had already finished the work. That's residue. It is what remains so you can exercise what God deposited. And when you faint, when you want to quit, when you feel like you're dying but you're still here—He is saying, "Be conscious. Align. Flow through it. Use what I gave you." Residue is not a punishment; it is training ground. It proves the reason He trusted you with power in the first place.

Consciousness requires you to know yourself—the good, the bad, and the ugly—so that you can rise in true peace. Healing is good, but wholeness is better. Wholeness means you flow with God when you like His decisions and when you don't. Wholeness means you are not just patched up, you are made complete. And consciousness teaches you that He is your only source of true strength. You stop working against Him and start working with Him. That is not theory, that is lived scripture. That is survival turned into testimony.

Your soul cry must become: "Make me aware, Lord." Not just aware of others, not just aware of systems, but aware of roots and not only harvest. I'll pause here—because this is where the shift happens. Too many settle for judging fruit while ignoring what feeds it. Consciousness heals you of abandonment, betrayal, and all the hidden seeds of brokenness because you stop looking only at harvest—you learn to discern the root. It's not just what's on top of the ground that matters. Anyone can look at a harvest and judge by sight, but what's underneath tells the greater story. Roots reveal more than fruit ever will.

Roots tell you about longevity—whether what you see will last or if it will wither the moment heat comes. Roots tell you about strength—whether the harvest can endure storms and drought or if it's shallow and fragile. Roots tell you about truth—whether the fruit is authentic or artificial, whether it's fed by living water or poisoned wells. Roots tell you about stability—whether the tree is planted by rivers of living water or standing weak in shifting sand. Consciousness opens your eyes to this unseen realm. It trains you not to be fooled by appearances but to discern the unseen strength beneath the soil. Because what's hidden is what's holding. What's beneath is what decides the harvest above.

Consciousness teaches you to rejoice even when circumstances resist joy, because awareness reveals joy that is not emotion but alignment. It steadies you with balance, a moderation that is not weakness but wisdom. It frees you from the grip of worry, because everything belongs in prayer, supplication, and thanksgiving. From that posture, peace comes—not a peace that makes sense to the mind, but a peace that guards the mind and steadies the heart. Consciousness looks up and sees the sky as a sermon, the sun as discipline, the moon as reminder. Day after day pours out speech, night after night reveals knowledge. Awareness catches what the distracted miss—the consistency of creation is an instruction manual for the soul. Consciousness shifts your appetite from the sweetness of gold and honey to the sweetness of His truth. It trains your taste so that what is eternal becomes more desirable than what glitters for a moment. And this is why discipline matters, because desire can be taught and realigned until your soul craves what your spirit was born for. Consciousness also welcomes warning. To be awake before God is to see not only fruit but the roots that produced it. Awareness uncovers hidden faults and presumptuous sins. It pulls you back from arrogance, rescues you from blind spots, and keeps you from being ruled by flesh. And in living this way—aligned, awake, aware—there is great reward: stability, innocence, wholeness.

Consciousness causes you to sit and listen. It teaches you to let God work things through you before you rush to speak them out. Without consciousness, you risk releasing words that you later have to retract—and retraction leaves people in limbo. What if someone never lives long enough to hear your correction? What if someone moves forward on what you said, only to find out it was your instability speaking and not God's revelation? Consciousness makes you wait. It makes you sit with your inconsistency, your decision-making, your inner wrestling, until what you carry has been tested in the fire of His voice. Consciousness is awareness not just of the beginning of a thing, but of the end. To me, this feels like a wedding ceremony—the vows are not proven on the first day, but over a lifetime. The true wedding with the Lord is not only at the altar of our first yes, but at the endurance of our last yes. Some things must be tested and proved before we put the weight of full investment on them. That is not doubt, it is integrity. It is credibility. It is the patience of a generation that desperately needs a revival of both. Consciousness is what gives weight to your word, because you didn't rush it, you let God mature it. That is good news. That is what will save not only your witness, but the faith of those who are watching you live it out.

Consciousness lets you leave all of the thinking to a sovereign God and receive the application that belongs to you. It is not your job to solve the infinite—it is your job to apply what He gives you. Consciousness produces an inner earth, an ecosystem of order and obedience within you. And when the inner earth is aligned, it begins to echo outward. Agreements are made in your spirit that ripple into agreements across nations. Alignment within births alignment without. And if we could ever get to that type of consciousness—where every believer allows God to think and we simply apply, where inner earths are healed and whole—then nations would see revival, unity would become reality, and the Kingdom would become visible in the earth.

And this is where I leave you with a charge: rise in consciousness until your roots are deep, your vision is clear, and your spirit is steady. May every hidden place in you be made whole, every scattered thought be brought into alignment, every fainting place find the strength to stand again. I declare over you that you will not settle for surface fruit but will press into roots; you will not waste power but will use residue; you will not confuse childishness with childlikeness but will walk in wonder and wisdom; you will not fight against God's math but will trust His equations. May peace that passes understanding guard you, may warnings rescue you, may discipline shape you, and may your inner earth become so aligned that it sets agreements across nations. This is your commissioning: to live conscious, to rise aware, to walk whole. Go forward knowing that strength with sight is destiny fulfilled.

"Awareness awakens the eyes, but reason steadies the steps."

Now that you are awake in consciousness, you cannot simply stop at awareness. To see is one thing; to understand the reason is another. Consciousness calls you to rise with clarity, but clarity must be coupled with purpose. This is your charge: do not just wake up—walk forward. Do not only recognize what is happening—realize why it is happening. For the rise is not sustained by sight alone. The rise is sustained by reason. And as you step into that reason, you will find yourself clothed, planted, and lifted—covered by the garment of praise, rooted as a seed of promise, and strengthened to soar as the eagle God has called you to be.

She Rise: Find the Reason

"Reason is not always found in the moment—it is revealed in the making. When sight fails, reason becomes the map that faith follows."

We do not always understand the weight of a step while we are taking it. Some seasons are confusing, some moments feel wasted, and some valleys seem endless. But reason is not always immediate; it is often hidden inside the process, waiting to unfold in due time. When our eyes cannot see, faith steadies us, reminding us that there is purpose even in the shadows. Faith carries us where sight cannot, and in the end, it leads us straight into the reason we thought we had lost.

There comes a moment in every rise where the question is not "how" but "why." She does not rise only to prove she can, nor simply to show her strength—she rises because somewhere in the pressing there is a reason. And it is that reason which turns empty steps into meaningful strides. Romans 8:28 tells us, "And we know that all things work together for good to them that love God, to them who are the called according to his purpose." Notice, it doesn't say some things, or only the easy things—it says all things. That means even the heartbreak, the setback, the detour, and the delay are being braided into purpose. The struggle becomes a seam in the garment of destiny. The tears become water for the soil of tomorrow's joy.

But how do you "know" when you don't see it? The text says, "And we know." That knowing is not sight—it is trust. It is not evidence—it is faith. It is the courage to walk even when the reason is still hidden.

> *"Awareness without purpose is like sight without direction—clarity with nowhere to go."*

And so much of the journey with God is not about knowing every answer, but about holding onto the truth that there is one.

Some steps do not make sense while we are walking them. Some feel wasted, like circling the same wilderness over and over again. Yet, Ecclesiastes 3 reminds us that "to every thing there is a season, and a time to every purpose under the heaven." What feels like delay may actually be divine alignment. What feels like wasted time may actually be preparation. Joseph knew this kind of mystery. Betrayed by his brothers, sold into slavery, forgotten in prison—none of those steps looked like purpose. And yet, at the appointed time, every betrayal and every delay positioned him to save a nation. His rise came because he did not despise the steps he could not understand.

I have found that the same principle is true in my own life. For me, this is where I lean into the Word of God not as theory but as truth. I actually believe what it says. And so when trials, temptations, oppression, depression, and suppression come, I know that what my eyes see is only part of the story. The scripture tells me to put on the garment of praise for the spirit of heaviness, and that is exactly what I do. When heaviness has tries to sit on me, I have praised myself into joy, because joy is not based on condition. I have also learned to embrace God as Omnibenevolent—a word we rarely use, yet one that carries the weight of His eternal nature. We often say, "God is good all the time, and all the time God is good," but we reduce it to a cliché without ever exploring the depth of its meaning. To say God is omnibenevolent is to declare that He is Holy, wholly, eternally, and unchangingly good, even when situations and circumstances do not feel good. It forces us to acknowledge the reality of evil in the world, but also the sovereignty of a God who remains good at all times.

His goodness is not occasional, it is essential, and as the psalmist declared, "O taste and see that the Lord is good: blessed is the man that trusteth in him" (Psalm 34:8). We cannot limit the word "good" to describe Him only when things are working for us or pleasing us. The manifestation of His goodness is exhibited in every essence of our life, shaping the cadence of our total environment. That understanding should signify the depth of our worship.

We must understand that praise is not just our outward expression of worship. Praise is the posture of speaking well of God—acknowledging His character, His goodness, and His sovereignty even when circumstances suggest otherwise. Praise is agreement with who He is, not just gratitude for what He has done. And because of that, praise is not weak or shallow—it is power. It is the power of God on the inside of me, fulfilling the promise of Isaiah 61:3 that God gives "beauty for ashes, the oil of joy for mourning, the garment of praise for the spirit of heaviness."

That power becomes the lens of what I call sight beyond sight. It is the ability to see God's goodness when the surface looks dark, to trace His hand when I cannot explain His plan. Sight beyond sight lets me stand in situations that make no earthly sense, yet still declare that God is good. It is seeing not only what is, but what it is becoming under His sovereign hand. It is choosing to believe that even in the confusion, goodness is present, reason is unfolding, and joy is already mine. This is why Habakkuk could say, "Although the fig tree shall not blossom, neither shall fruit be in the vines… Yet I will rejoice in the Lord, I will joy in the God of my salvation" (Habakkuk 3:17–18).

Joy is not something I wait for when things get better; joy is something I carry because God is with me. That is how I rise even when the steps don't make sense , and why David could say with confidence, "Thou wilt shew me the path of life:

in thy presence is fulness of joy; at thy right hand there are pleasures for evermore" (Psalm 16:11).

There are also some lessons that life itself cannot teach us, no matter how much we read, study, or prepare. They are too deep to be reached by ordinary instruction. These lessons only come through the press of experience. James 1:2–4 tells us, "My brethren, count it all joy when ye fall into divers temptations; knowing this, that the trying of your faith worketh patience. But let patience have her perfect work, that ye may be perfect and entire, wanting nothing." Experience is the teacher that time employs. If life does not teach you, time will insist on it. The test you keep facing again and again is not because God is cruel but because maturity demands repetition until the lesson becomes part of you. Some doors will not open until the lesson is lived, not just learned.

That has been the story of my becoming. This is how I learned to see with what I call sight beyond sight. Not that my situations ever felt joyful in themselves—pain was still pain, disappointment still stung, dysfunction still left its mark. Yet through every dilemma and every dysfunction, I was graced with wisdom, tools, and strategy for the betterment of my life. What looked like an ending often became an opening. What felt like defeat became the soil of victory. And time taught me what life never could: that joy is not a visitor, it is a resident. When you live with sight beyond sight, you recognize that there is a reason within even the hardest seasons.

To enjoy the journey is not to pretend that every part of it is enjoyable. It means that even in confusion, you choose to trust the Author of the story. Paul wrote in Philippians 1:6, "Being confident of this very thing, that he which hath begun a good work in you will perform it until the day of Jesus Christ." If He started it, He will finish it. The rise may not be smooth, but it will be sure. The climb may feel steep, but it is shaping you for the view at the top.

This is why I can enjoy the journey. Because I have learned to look at life with joyful eyesight—not denying what I see, but choosing to see with a greater sight. Every rise has a reason. Every hardship carries a hidden seed. And when I view my climb through sight beyond sight, I don't just survive the steps—I find the reason in them. I enjoy the journey not because every moment is pleasurable but because every moment is purposeful. My joy does not come from what I feel, it comes from what I know: that God is faithful, that His Word is true, and that nothing is wasted.

She rises not because she understands everything but because she believes there is a reason for everything. The hidden pieces of her story are not wasted—they are weaving her into someone she could not have become otherwise. What she could not learn naturally, she has been forced to learn through experience. And what life refused to teach her, time itself has whispered until she heard. She has come to know that even when her eyes cannot see, her spirit can still discern. That is the gift of sight beyond sight—the ability to recognize that purpose is present even in pain, that wisdom is waiting even in loss, and that joy is available even in sorrow.

So she wears her garment of praise, because heaviness cannot hold her when worship clothes her. She plants her seeds of faith, because what feels buried will one day break through the soil with harvest. And she spreads her wings like the eagle, because those who wait upon the Lord shall renew their strength, they shall mount up, they shall run and not be weary, they shall walk and not faint. The garment keeps her covered, the seed keeps her growing, and the eagle keeps her soaring. These three together define her reason, her resilience, and her rise.

And so I declare: I rise with reason. I rise with trust. I rise with joy in the journey. Every step is working together for my good. Nothing is wasted. My climb has meaning, and my reason will be revealed in due time.

Lord, open my eyes to see beyond the step I'm on. Teach me the hidden reason, even if only in part. Strengthen my faith when the journey feels unclear and help me count it all joy as patience shapes me. Let me rise not only in strength but in wisdom, finding the reason in every moment You allow.

Rise knowing that God's goodness is unchanging, let praise be your power, live with sight beyond sight, and carry joy as your constant companion—this is how you rise with reason. Now go forth with confidence, refusing to be defined by what you see in the moment, and stand assured that every step holds a reason. When heaviness comes, wear your garment of praise. When hope feels buried, plant your seed of faith. When strength feels spent, spread your eagle's wings. You are not rising aimlessly—you are rising with reason. And that reason will carry you into the fullness of who God designed you to be.

"When purpose ignites within a person, even silence starts a revolution."

Revolution begins the moment a soul decides to live louder than its fear. It doesn't always shout—it often starts in silence, in that quiet decision to no longer be ruled by what once held you back. When purpose ignites within a person, even silence starts a revolution. What follows isn't rebellion, it's release. It's the sound of someone stepping into who they were always meant to be, unafraid, unhidden, and undeniably free.

She Rise in Revolution

*"Grace is the revolution. Surrender is the weapon.
Christ is the victory."*

Sin is overrated. Not because it is imaginary, not because its wounds are not real, but because Jesus already crushed its power. Somewhere along the way we learned to preach sin louder than salvation, to magnify condemnation louder than transformation, and to measure identity by failure instead of by the finished work on the cross. I rise to say plainly that sin has been dethroned. It is no longer the headline of your story. Christ is.

You may not think this is part of my story, but it is, because part of my calling is to bring clarity to the fuzzy places in people's lives. I have stood in the fog of condemnation. I have measured myself against standards that were never God's. I have bowed to a perfection that the flesh could never produce. The Lord taught me the revolution begins when we stop chasing the image of flawlessness and start embracing the power of grace.

We need to define sin as more than the things we dislike or the behaviors we choose to tolerate. Sin is not just the "big ones" we shame others for, while excusing the "small ones" we secretly live with. Sin is every place where humanity has stepped outside of God's design. From what the world calls the worst offense to what people excuse as the least offense, the root is the same separation from God. That is why the focus on sin is overrated. When you live measuring yourself by a sliding scale of sins, you miss the only truth that matters: the power of the work of Christ.

The psalmist said, Behold, I was shaped in iniquity; and in sin did my mother conceive me (Psalm 51:5). That was the world's starting point for all of us—born in sin, shaped in iniquity, carrying the imprint of a fallen nature. But Christ came to restore what sin distorted. The power of His blood pulled us back into God's original design. Where sin had written one story, the Spirit has authored a new one. Where iniquity had shaped our lives, grace now reshapes us in righteousness.

This is the real revolution: to stop living from what made you and to start living from how God created you. To stop circling in cycles of speculation and questioning, and to rise into trust and obedience. To destroy the identity the world forced on you and embrace the identity God breathed into you. When you live from Spirit, you no longer rehearse sin as your headline—you walk in life as your testimony.

Read the apostle Paul and you will see your own heart reflected. For the good that I would I do not: but the evil which I would not, that I do (Romans 7:19). Paul did not pretend away the tension between flesh and spirit. He named it, he grieved it, and he pointed beyond it to the answer. The revolution is not denying that we wrestle. The revolution is naming the wrestling and refusing to let it be the final word. Sin will not have dominion over you: for ye are not under the law, but under grace (Romans 6:14). That is the posture of a soul who knows its Redeemer.

At a young age I learned to stop policing my imperfections and to start stewarding my heart. Perfection was a prison I could never escape, no matter how hard I tried. Every flaw, every stumble, every word spoken out of turn became another chain around me. But God whispered that He was not asking me to be flawless, He was asking me to be faithful. He was not measuring me by how few mistakes I made, but by how fully I surrendered to His Spirit. That revelation shifted me from chasing image to cultivating intimacy, from judging myself by rules to yielding myself to relationship.

When I stopped policing my imperfections, I discovered grace. When I started stewarding my heart, I discovered transformation. It was not about ignoring sin—it was about dethroning it, about refusing to let it be the lens through which I saw my life. I realized that the Spirit was not waiting for me to be spotless before He moved; He was moving in me so that my spots would lose their stain. My calling became clearer, my walk steadier, and my rise inevitable—not because I perfected myself, but because I allowed His perfection to work in me.

Do not let the enemy trap you in cycles of guilt. The adversary loves for you to rehearse your sin until you forget your Savior. But God says turn and live. Keep growing. Keep cleansing your heart. Keep surrendering. Sanctification is not an instant erasure of struggle; it is the Spirit's patient work of making you more like Christ day by day. The presence of temptation is not proof you are failing; it is proof you are alive in Christ because only the living engage in a war between flesh and Spirit. The Spirit is winning in you even when you still feel the fight.

Keep your worship. Keep your praise in whatever state you are in. Faithful praise in the night is the seedbed for dawn. The one who is faithful will complete the work. You are His masterpiece. The more you highlight Christ the less you magnify yourself. Rise in Him. It is not by might, nor by power, but by my spirit, saith the Lord of hosts (Zechariah 4:6). When you choose worship over worry and praise over paralysis you position yourself for breakthrough. So let your heart be a sanctuary of thanksgiving even while you are being repaired. Let your mouth declare the victory that your feet have not fully walked yet and watch the Spirit make the pathway real.

This revolution will cause you to go higher and deeper at the same time. You cannot ascend to true authority on the surface of a heart that is shallow. You cannot go higher without going deeper. Depth is the crucible where character is formed and calling is clarified. The Spirit will take you into places of hidden work so that your public rise is steady and unshakable. When the foundations are deep, the storms will not uproot you. So dive into the secret place, press into obedience, and let the Wellspring of life fill you until your overflow becomes the world's water.

Hear me. This is not a soft apology for sin. This is a prophetic dismantling of its false throne. We will speak of sin with clarity and not with caricature. We will name transgression and call for repentance. Yet we will not make the naming the end of the story. The cross is the end of the story. When He said, It is finished, He meant finished. The work is accomplished. Your life now is to live from that accomplished work, to let the Spirit complete what the cross declared, to walk daily in the victory purchased for you.

So rise. Rise from the fog of accusation. Rise from the habit of shrinking. Rise from the heavy weight of legalism. Rise into worship, into obedience, into trust. Rise not because you have achieved a spotless record but because you have surrendered to a spotless Savior. Rise because the work of Christ is powerful enough to remake you. Rise because praise will carry you through the night into tomorrow. Rise because you are His masterpiece and the revolution lives in your heart.

This is my final rise in this book, but it will not be the last rise of my life. I am not closing these pages with a whisper of defeat but with the sound of a revolution. I stand as living proof that sin does not have the last word, shame does not write the final sentence, and condemnation does not decide the ending. Christ does. And because Christ does, I rise.

I rise not because I have never stumbled but because I refuse to stay down. I rise not because I am flawless but because I am fearless in grace. I rise not because sin has vanished from this world but because the Savior has conquered it for me. And every time I turn toward Him, every time I let my heart be cleansed, every time I surrender my will to His Spirit, I live again.

I declare I will not be held captive by the voice of condemnation. I will not bow at the altar of shame. I will not measure my worth by perfection. I rise in the finished work of Christ. I rise with a heart being cleansed daily, a mind being renewed constantly, and a spirit being strengthened eternally. I rise not in my own strength but in His.

Pray with me: Lord, I thank You that sin has no dominion over me. I thank You that You take no pleasure in death but that You rejoice in life. Cleanse my heart, renew my mind, and draw me closer to the fullness of Your Spirit. Teach me to rise not in fear but in faith, not in striving but in surrender. Fill me with fresh oil, pour over me with grace, and let my strength be perfected in You. In Jesus' name, Amen.

Beyond the Rise
(The Journey Continues)

To the One Who's Rising

"You don't have to feel ready. You just have to refuse to bow. This rise is still yours."

You. Yes, you. The one who's still rising while weeping. The one who endured betrayal and survived the storm. The one they overlooked, misunderstood, underestimated, and blamed—but you're still rising.

Let this be your reminder:
You were never supposed to break—you were destined to build.
You were never just supposed to suffer—you were called to shift.
Your story isn't fragile—it's fire-wrapped wisdom. Your scars are scrolls. Your name has weight. Your breath is proof that purpose still has plans for you.

Because when you rise, hell loses its bet.

When you rise, history rewrites itself.
When you rise, systems get nervous and heaven gets louder.
When you rise, the next generation watches and remembers how.

Don't apologize for your oil.

Don't wait for them to understand.

Let your fruit speak. Let your fire guide. Let your silence teach.
Live. Learn. Weep. Rename. Get up.
Build. Burn the excuses. Breathe again.
Don't settle. Don't shrink. Don't stop.

You're not just surviving—you're becoming a blueprint.

You are the instruction manual navigating the storm.

So rise in strategy. Rise in strength. Rise in silence. Rise with scars.

And when you can't rise loud—rise still.

Because She Rise. And because she rise—everything shifts.

Now that you've walked through every chapter, wrestled through the hard truths, and risen through the revelation...it's time to anchor what you've received.

These final declarations, truths, and life creeds are not just words—they are tools. They are your mirror, your compass, and your mantle.

Read them slowly. Return to them often. Let them be a reminder of who you are becoming and the legacy you're called to leave. This is more than the end of a book—it's the beginning of your next level.

I Rise – A Personal Declaration of Becoming

- I rise—not because it was easy,
- but because quitting was never my portion.
- I rise—through silence, through sorrow,
- through betrayal, through becoming.
- I rise—not to prove a point,
- but to fulfill a purpose.
- I rise—while weeping.
- I rise—with strategy.
- I rise—in obedience.
- I rise without applause.
- I rise because I am called.
- I rise because I am chosen.
- I rise because I carry oil.
- I rise—not in my own strength,
- but in the strength of the One who sustained me.
- I rise from what tried to bury me.
- I rise from what should have broken me.
- I rise with wisdom in my mouth
- and fire in my hands.
- I rise with the blueprint.
- I rise as the evidence.
- I rise for those who haven't yet found their voice.

- Because I was never meant to stay down.
  - And the odds?
  - They lost when I got back up.
  - I rise with healing.
  - I rise with power.
  - I rise with joy restored.
- I rise—and because I rise, everything shifts.

I Rise Whole

I rise not just to be seen—but to be sent.
I rise not just to be strong—but to be surrendered.
I rise with healed hands and a steady heart.
I rise carrying oil, carrying truth, carrying fire.
No part of me was wasted.
No season of my life was for nothing.
Every scar became a scroll.
Every wound birthed wisdom.
I rise not by volume—but by vision.
Not by applause—but by assignment.
I rise in rhythm with heaven.
I rise in reverence and restoration.
I rise because God spoke.
And I say yes.
She Rise. And because she rise—everything shifts.

A Final Guardrail: Protect What's Been Poured

You can't allow empty people, especially those who choose to stay empty and never take the time to allow God to plug their holes, to empty you. I am all for extending yourself to help those in need. I've lived it—sacrificing my very being for people I truly tried to love and help.

But there comes a point when you realize some people will keep blowing out your match, while still expecting you to burn for them. They'll drain your energy, demand your light, and disregard your efforts—and yet expect you to keep showing up whole. That's when you have to stop and evaluate the situation. Because your fire was never meant to be mishandled. Not your strength, not your clarity, not your anointing. Not your wholeness. Your wholeness is not up for negotiation. Your progress is not a peace offering. Your divine refill is not meant to be wasted on people who refuse to heal, grow, or align.

You were not raised, rebuilt, restored, or reclaimed to become the emotional trash can or spiritual drip line for those who don't honor the cost of your becoming. Just because you carry oil does not mean you are required to pour it into broken barrels. You are not their rescue if they won't even receive revelation. You are not required to carry people who choose to live in cycles and call it warfare. Kingdom discernment says: Don't let what you've been filled with be siphoned by who refuses to be whole.

This is your reminder to guard your gates, protect your oil, and preserve you, and your wholeness. You are not their God. You are not their guilt trip. You are a vessel. Rise accordingly—and wisely.

From My Rise to Yours
A Closing Letter to You

My end was a transformational strategist.

Yours might look different.

Whatever it is, just fulfill it.

Whether it's a business, a classroom, a family, a movement, a message, a healing space, or simply a whole, restored life… walk it out with fire in your bones and truth in your steps.

Don't let pain become your ceiling.

Don't let people become your permission.

And don't let the past narrate your next.

Find your strength.

Stand in it.

Live within the confidence of your journey—not anyone else's.

You don't owe them an explanation.

You owe Heaven your yes.

You've survived.

Now it's time to build.

Because you, too, rise.

And that… is enough.

With love, oil, and bold expectation,

~Dr. Sherrise C. Cohen-Hooks

She Rise.

To Be Continued…

In the work.

In the healing.

In the rising.

She Rise.

"Being confident of this very thing, that he which hath begun a good work in you will perform it until the day of Jesus Christ." Philippians 1:6

May your rise never end, because the God who began it will finish it.

A Final Whisper for the Hungry Heart

If you've made it to this point, something in you is rising. And as you rise, there will be moments when you need to go back—not to what hurt you, but to what heals you. That's where the Word comes in. Not just the words of this book, but the Word of God—timeless, holy, anchored in truth. The scriptures that follow aren't here to preach *at* you. They are here to *walk* with you. To confirm, to strengthen, to remind you that everything God is birthing in you is backed by eternal breath. Open them. Pray through them. Study them. Let them speak where silence lingers. Let them carry you deeper.

You rise—and the Word walks with you.

References for Deeper Study & Confirmation

Before you is a full listing of biblical references connected to each chapter of She Rise: A Book of Strength. These scriptures are gathered not just for confirmation, but for continuation — so you may carry the Word deeper into your healing, faith, and obedience. As you revisit them, let them open fresh revelation. As you pray them, let them stir new strength. And as you live them, let them become the proof that your rise is not in word only, but in Spirit and in truth.

SHE RISE: WILDERNESS – PART I: THE PROCESS WAS THE WILDERNESS

Deuteronomy 8:2   Exodus 16:4   Matthew 4:1

Mark 1:12–13   Hosea 2:14   Numbers 14:33–34

Isaiah 35:1   Revelation 12:6   Jeremiah 2:2

SHE RISE IN SILENCE

Psalm 46:10   1 Kings 19:12   Isaiah 30:15   Habakkuk 2:20

Lamentations 3:26   Zephaniah 1:7   Amos 5:13   Ecclesiastes 3:7   Psalm 62:1

SHE RISE WHILE WEEPING

Psalm 30:5   John 11:35   Psalm 56:8   Revelation 21:4
Jeremiah 31:16   Psalm 6:8   Luke 7:38   Isaiah 25:8
Psalm 34:18

SHE RISE WITH STRATEGY

Proverbs 16:3   Luke 14:28   Joshua 1:8   Ecclesiastes 3:1
Nehemiah 2:17–18   Proverbs 21:5   Matthew 10:16
Isaiah 32:8   1 Corinthians 9:26

SHE RISE: FROM STORM TO ENDURANCE, FORMED LIKE A SNOWFLAKE

Isaiah 40:31   James 1:2–4   Romans 5:3–4

2 Corinthians 4:17   Mark 4:39–41   Psalm 107:29
Matthew 8:26   Hebrews 12:1–2   1 Peter 5:10

BECAUSE SHE RISE HEALED

Jeremiah 30:17   Isaiah 53:5   Malachi 4:2   Psalm 147:3
1 Peter 2:24   Exodus 15:26   Matthew 9:22
Psalm 103:2–3   Proverbs 17:22

SHE RISE IN MORPH: HONORING THE HIDDEN TRANSFORMATIONS

2 Corinthians 5:17   Romans 12:2   Isaiah 43:19   Philippians 1:6   Ezekiel 36:26   Galatians 6:15   Colossians 3:10   John 15:2   Job 23:10

BECAUSE SHE RISE, SHE DEFEATED THE ODDS

Romans 8:31   1 John 5:4   Judges 6:15–16   Philippians 4:13   Isaiah 54:17   Psalm 18:29   Deuteronomy 20:4   2 Corinthians 4:8–9   Micah 7:8

SHE RISE: THE ANATOMY OF MY BECOMING

Jeremiah 1:5   Psalm 139:13–14   Ephesians 2:10   Romans 8:29–30   Galatians 1:15   Job 10:8–9   Isaiah 64:8   Philippians 3:12   2 Timothy 1:9

SHE RISE WITH TOOLS

Ephesians 6:11   Hebrews 4:12   2 Timothy 3:16–17   2 Corinthians 10:4   Isaiah 54:16–17   Luke 10:19   Psalm 18:34   Proverbs 4:7   Colossians 3:16

BORNDAGE: BREAKING BIRTH-BOUND CHAINS

John 8:36   Isaiah 61:1   Galatians 5:1   Romans 6:6
Exodus 6:6   Psalm 107:14   2 Corinthians 3:17   Micah 2:13   Colossians 1:13

DEPTH OF THE RISE

Psalm 42:7   1 Corinthians 2:10   Ephesians 3:18–19
Colossians 2:7   Proverbs 20:5   Psalm 36:6
Isaiah 55:8–9   Romans 11:33   Job 12:22

HARD CHOICES AND HOLY RETURNS: SHE RISE TRUTH

Deuteronomy 30:19   Ruth 1:16–17   Matthew 16:24
Hebrews 12:11   Joshua 24:15   Luke 22:42
2 Timothy 2:3   Malachi 3:7   Jeremiah 3:22

SHE RISE WITH VOICE

Jeremiah 20:9   Acts 4:20   Isaiah 58:1
Proverbs 31:8–9   Exodus 4:12   Psalm 81:10   Matthew 10:20
Romans 10:14   Revelation 12:11

SHE RISE WORD OF FIRE: YOUR EMOTIONS ARE NOT YOUR ALTAR

Jeremiah 23:29	Ephesians 4:26	Galatians 5:22–23
James 1:19–20	Leviticus 6:12–13	Hebrews 12:29
1 Peter 4:12	Proverbs 25:28	Colossians 3:8

THE RISE OF OBEDIENCE: SEEING WITHOUT SIGHT

1 Samuel 15:22 2 Corinthians 5:7 Isaiah 1:19

Romans 1:5 Hebrews 11:8 John 14:23 Deuteronomy 28:1

Philippians 2:8 Luke 11:28

WHAT RISING LOOKS LIKE ON EMPTY

2 Corinthians 12:9–10	Isaiah 40:29	Matthew 11:28–30
Philippians 4:12–13	Psalm 63:1	Habakkuk 3:17–18
Lamentations 3:22–23	1 Kings 17:12–14	John 6:35

SHE RISE THROUGH THE WILDERNESS – PART II

Exodus 13:21	Hosea 2:14	Mark 1:13
Deuteronomy 32:10	Psalm 78:52	Isaiah 43:19–20
Ezekiel 20:35	Nehemiah 9:19	Revelation 17:3

FROM WILDERNESS TO WIND: THE RISE DOESN'T END, IT DEEPENS

Ezekiel 37:9–10   John 3:8   Acts 2:2–4   Isaiah 40:13

Job 37:9–10   Psalm 135:7   Zechariah 4:6

2 Kings 2:11   John 20:22

SHE RISE LESSONS LEARNED

Proverbs 24:16   James 1:5   Psalm 119:71

Romans 15:4   Job 5:17   Hebrews 5:8

2 Corinthians 4:17   Micah 6:8   Psalm 90:12

SHE RISE WITH STRENGTH

Nehemiah 8:10   Isaiah 40:31   Philippians 4:13

Ephesians 6:10   Psalm 27:1   2 Timothy 2:1   Joshua 1:9

Habakkuk 3:19   Psalm 18:32

SHE RISE IN CONSCIOUSNESS

Romans 12:2   2 Corinthians 10:5   Philippians 2:5

Colossians 3:2   Psalm 19:14   Isaiah 26:3   Proverbs 23:7

Matthew 22:37   1 Peter 1:13

SHE RISE: FIND THE REASON

Romans 8:28	Ecclesiastes 3:11	Habakkuk 2:3
2 Timothy 1:9	Genesis 50:20	Jeremiah 29:11
1 Peter 5:10	Psalm 138:8	John 9:3

SHE RISE IN REVOLUTION

Daniel 11:32	Acts 17:6	Revelation 12:11
Matthew 11:12	Jeremiah 1:10	Luke 4:18–19
Acts 4:31	2 Corinthians 10:4–5	Psalm 149:6–9

About the Author

Dr. S.C. Cohen-Hooks is a transformational strategist, apostolic voice, spiritual architect, and teacher of truth whose life and ministry embody the sacred rhythm of rising. She is the founder of Reclaimed for Christ Ministries and Kingdom Vision Eternal Impact Church, and serves as the visionary leader of The Church of ACTS: From Word to Life and Believers to Kingdom Association. As CEO of Elevated Connection LLC, she has spent more than 20 years building dreams, advancing healing, and creating pathways of development that touch both the spiritual and practical dimensions of life.

For over two decades, Dr. Sherrise has been a vessel of healing, transformation, and truth—hosting conferences, facilitating deliverance-intensive workshops, leading inner healing seminars, and creating prophetic spaces for wholeness and renewal. Her teachings stir deep conviction, unlock identity, and birth sustainable spiritual growth.

She Rise is her first published release, but it carries the weight of many unspoken altars, private sacrifices, and public breakthroughs. She writes as one who has lived the stretch, survived the silence, and still chose surrender. Through every page, she invites you to rise not in pretense, but in power.

Dr. Sherrise's voice echoes through pulpits, radio airwaves, healing sessions, and intimate moments of counsel. Whether you encounter her through a book, a sermon, or a prayer, you'll quickly realize—this is not performance. This is presence.

Many people ask why it took her so long to publish. Her reply is simple: the appointed time. She was always writing, working, building, and storing, but first she invested her life in her greatest assignment—her three biological children. For more than 30 years, she has poured into her marriage and her home, watching the fruitfulness of God's faithfulness manifest in their lives. Because of that lived investment, her words are not just inspiration, but embodied knowledge and undeniable truth, carried by the evidence of fruit.

Beyond the platform, she remains a wife of more than 30 years, the devoted mother of three biological children, and more. She is a woman who treasures family as both legacy and ministry. Her marriage, her children, and her personal journey ground her message in lived reality, making her words not only prophetic but profoundly human. Her life is a testimony that rising is not only possible—it is generational.

She Rise.

www.ingramcontent.com/pod-product-compliance
Lightning Source LLC
Chambersburg PA
CBHW070757230426
43665CB00017B/2396